To Whom Shall We Go?

"This is a book like no other! It offers a deep spirituality of hope when we are stuck in a crisis. But it does much more. These authors woo us into the presence of the God of hope through ancient and modern spiritual practices. . . . A rich breviary for today and tomorrow. Read it and learn to pray."

—**R. Paul Stevens**, Professor Emeritus, Regent College, and author of *Down-to-Earth Spirituality*

"In a time when we are forced to live in suspension, out comes this book of signposts on how to navigate through the deep and dark ambiguities of the current pandemic. . . . This book is a most helpful companion for the journey, a precious keepsake we can take with us as we struggle for insight, for ways of critiquing systems and structures we have come to accept as normal because regnant with power and routinized."

—**Melba Padilla Maggay**, president, Institute for Studies in Asian Church and Culture

"Covid-19 has swept like a scythe through the world. What was normal in every aspect of life in every part of the globe has been impacted. Here is a welcome potpourri of thoughtful reflections and prayers, along with questions for groups, based around the profound wisdom of the Beatitudes. It is an excellent and timely resource for this extraordinary time of social disruption, spiritual disorientation, and deep personal grief."

—**Tim Costello**, executive director of Micah, Australia

"This book is a challenging gift. . . . The authors reflect on the Covid crisis through the lens of their own spirituality, their reflections on the Beatitudes, and their spiritual readings of the sages of the church. . . . *To Whom Shall We Go* is provocative, eliciting careful thought, reflection, prayer, and action, teaching us to broaden our hearts and strengthen our commitment to each other and to God."

—**Alan Gijsbers**, former president, Healthserve Australia

"This is a book for those seeking substance for their souls. The authors come from different disciplines but share a strong but light-touch commitment to spiritual direction. This is expressed in a sustained engagement with our interior lives. Prayers, poems and liturgies bring reflectivity to the chapters. A substantial bibliography and helpful indexes round it off. A solidly satisfying meal for the whole person—truly a blessing."

—**Gordon Preece**, director of Ethos: Evangelical Alliance Centre for Christianity and Society

To Whom Shall We Go?

— Faith Responses in a Time of Crisis —

EDITED BY

Irene Alexander

AND

Christopher Brown

CASCADE *Books* • Eugene, Oregon

TO WHOM SHALL WE GO?
Faith Responses in a Time of Crisis

Cascade Books
An Imprint of Wipf and Stock Publishers
199 W. 8th Ave., Suite 3
Eugene, OR 97401

www.wipfandstock.com

PAPERBACK ISBN: 978-1-7252-8955-0
HARDCOVER ISBN: 978-1-7252-8956-7
EBOOK ISBN: 978-1-7252-8957-4

Cataloguing-in-Publication data:

Names: Alexander, Irene, editor. | Brown, Christopher, editor.

Title: To whom shall we go? : faith responses in a time of crisis / edited by Irene Alexander and Christopher Brown.

Description: Eugene, OR: Cascade Books, 2021 | Includes bibliographical references and index.

Identifiers: ISBN 978-1-7252-8955-0 (paperback) | ISBN 978-1-7252-8956-7 (hardcover) | ISBN 978-1-7252-8957-4 (ebook)

Subjects: LCSH: COVID-19 Pandemic 2020–2021. | Spirituality—Christianity. | Peace-building. | Social justice.

Classification: HM1121 .T60 2021 (print) | HM1121 (ebook)

05/05/21

To whom shall we go?
You have the words of eternal life,
and we have believed and have come to know
that You are the Holy One of God.[1]

1. Northumbria Community, *Celtic Daily Prayer*, 865.

Contents

Contributors

Dr. Irene Alexander has a background in psychology, missions, and tertiary education. Irene has taught counselling and spiritual companioning related courses in Brisbane, Australia, the Philippines, Myanmar, and Malaysia. Irene lives some of the year in the Philippines where she is adjunct faculty at Asian Theological Seminary and is part of Servants to Asia's Urban Poor. She also teaches at the Australian Catholic University and has written several books, mostly in the interface between spirituality and psychology, including: *Dancing with God; Practicing the Presence of Jesus; A Glimpse of the Kingdom in Academia; How Relationships Work.* Irene is a grandmother to five grandchildren, delighting in being part of the curiosity and openness of young minds growing up in a multicultural, multifaith world.

Christopher Basil Brown qualified in Psychology (MA, University of Sydney), Social Policy (MSc , London School of Economics), and Social Work (DipSocSt, University of Sydney). Chris taught social work at the University of Queensland (twenty-five years), and counseling/spiritual companioning at Christian Heritage College (twelve years). Now semi-retired, he offers spiritual direction (for the past twenty-three years), supervision, and has been a formator of spiritual directors. He is the author of *Guiding Gideon: Awakening to Life and Faith* and *Reflected Love: Companioning in the Way of Jesus*; and has written articles on Christian spirituality and spiritual direction.

Dr. Terry Gatfield is a retired academic, having taught in business disciplines in Australian and Asian Universities. He lives in Brisbane in a purpose-built home with a low carbon footprint on nine acres of land close to the city. He is an Anglican communicant and a Third Order Franciscan, a companion of the Celtic Northumbrian Community and a member of the Holy Scribblers writing fraternity. His passions are organic gardening, model steam engine building, coin collecting, furniture restoration, bee keeping, and writing. His life is optimized by working with his four children and ten grandchildren.

Dr. Athena E. Gorospe was born in Manila, Philippines, where she grew up in a city with big disparities between the rich and the poor. This developed her active compassion and commitment to the suffering and the marginalized, particularly women, the urban and rural poor, migrants, victims of natural disasters and extrajudicial killings, and persons deprived of liberty. Athena integrates advocacy work into her biblical scholarship. She is the author of an Asian commentary on *Judges* and *Narrative and Identity: An Ethical Reading of Exodus 4*. She has also written articles and edited volumes that show an interface between Scripture and current social realities, including *How Long, O Lord?: The Challenge and Promise of Reconciliation and Peace*. She is associate professor in biblical studies and director of the PhD Program in contextual theology at the Asian Theological Seminary in Manila, Philippines.

Dr. Tim McCowan is senior lecturer in spirituality at the University of Divinity, a spiritual director, a leader of silent retreats, and an ordained minister. He is also involved in the formation of spiritual directors at the Asian Theological Seminary in the Philippines. His PhD evaluated the Building Bridges in Schools Program, https://www.buildingbridges.org.au/ that he founded shortly after September 11 and then directed for twelve years. Prior to this he worked with Servants to Asia's Urban Poor in Manila for eight years. Tim is married to Mary and lives in Melbourne, where he is a member of a Baptist community.

Dr. Ross McKenzie is a Professor of Physics at the University of Queensland and a consultant for the International Fellowship of Evangelical Students. Ross enjoys writing two blogs: *Soli Deo Gloria: Thoughts on theology, science, and culture* (revelation4-11.blogspot.com) a blog related to his scientific research at condensedconcepts.blogspot.com. He is currently writing *Condensed Matter Physics: A Very Short Introduction*.

Dr. Paul Mercer is an experienced general practitioner, having worked in Brisbane for the past thirty-seven years. Paul, with his wife Katrina, is a member of the Uniting Church. Currently, he chairs the Board of Health Serve Australia, an international NGO seeking to make a contribution to health development internationally, and particularly in our COVID-19 context. He is also part of the Theology on Tap Brisbane team. Paul is a Life Member of the Royal Australian College of General Practitioners. He served as the chair of the College's Preventative and Community Medicine Committee from 1998 to 2001. He is an accredited general practice training supervisor, and for the past fourteen years has been the editor of *Luke's Journal*, an Australian Christian medical and dental journal.

Sarah L. Nicholl, LLB, MCS, is a retired solicitor who practiced law both in the United Kingdom and Canada. She also gained a Masters in Christian Studies at Regent College, Vancouver, with a focus on spiritual theology. She is currently a candidate for a PhD in the School of History and Philosophical Inquiry at the University of Queensland, Australia. Sarah currently lives in Vancouver, British Columbia, with her significant others: Alan, her husband; Joel, their son; and Skipper, their dog. For fun, Sarah enjoys long distance running, travelling, and entertaining.

Dr. Charles Ringma has taught in universities, colleges, and seminaries in Australia, Asia, and Canada. He is emeritus professor, Regent College, Vancouver, Canada. He is a Franciscan Tertiary and a companion of Northumbria Community, Brisbane. His many books on Christian spirituality include *Seek the Silences with Thomas Merton* and *Hear the Ancient Wisdom*. He is involved in justice issues and plants rain forest trees. Visit charlesringma.com and https://holyscribblers.blogspot.com

Preface

These times of crisis and of global change require of us that we engage with our deepest values, and the foundations of our Christian faith, to find purpose and integrity in how we respond individually and institutionally. How are we to live out our lives in prayerful and active participation with God's life and purposes amid the coronavirus pandemic and in its aftermath? How might we pray that God's kingdom will come on earth as it is in heaven, and renew our citizenship of both our heavenly and earthly kingdoms? We are being invited to live our lives in the midst of a dilemma heightened by the current crisis. What might shape the characteristic of the kingdom life we seek to live out as the pandemic and its after-effects creates societal upheaval and anxiety in our world?

It is the suggestion of this book to look towards the Sermon on the Mount, first at the person of Jesus, and then to his beatitudes. Though this is not a book specifically about the Beatitudes, they will be referenced throughout the chapters, as the basic scaffolding for this collection. There is mystery in their forming and shaping capacity, especially in the way the Beatitudes can become autobiographical, and this book reflects upon how they can orient and ground us for kingdom participation both within this time of crisis and beyond.

The authors of this book, most of whom form a group called the "holy" scribblers (holyscribblers.blogspot.com), come from diverse backgrounds: medicine, social work, theology, law, economics, physics, missions, psychology, and spiritual direction. They are a group of friends who have been writing about a theological, spiritual, and practical response to our times. They bring their diverse perspectives to the question of how to live a faith-filled response to times of crisis, using the Beatitudes as a framework for reflection.

We would like to especially acknowledge the editorial work of Charles Ringma and Karen Hollenbeck-Wuest, whose gifts have brought many books to birth.

Irene Alexander and Christopher Brown

Brisbane, Australia.
October 2020

Introduction

The worldwide pandemic has created a time for all of humanity to pause and reflect on the way we are living our lives as individuals, organizations, and nations. For those in the Christian tradition, who have Jesus' life, death, resurrection, and indwelling presence at the core of who they are, the task is to discern and attune to his Spirit in these troubling times. The question we face is how to live more intentionally as citizens of our earthly home as well as the kingdom of God. How are we to live prayerfully and reflectively, as well as responding actively to the needs of our world? Two imperatives are to become more attentive to the empowering narrative of Scripture, and to engage life more prayerfully. This is not so that we may become more pious. It is so that our friendship with God may deepen, and that we may more fully enter into the redemptive purposes of God for our upside-down world. Our wonderful, bruised, and threatened world is the place where we need to live out our intimacy with the God who seeks to restore all things.

The invitation is to respond to the Spirit's leading in the midst of turmoil. It is not always easy to know what should be done, as often this involves working alongside others, while being cognizant of the divine hand. We may try to do "much too much," as if everything depended on us. Sometimes we do the opposite and drop the ball. Finding a balance between giving and receiving, and making our contribution, while allowing others to make theirs, will always be a challenge for us. And this is made all the more demanding in times of crisis where we may question God, ourselves, and others. This is all the more complex when we seek to work this out in our relationship with God. What must we leave to God and what must we do are challenging questions. What is God's work and what is ours? How might we participate in God's life and purposes? What can we leave to others and to government? And what must we do at a personal level?

Because these questions become amplified due to the pandemic crisis, we as citizens of the kingdoms of heaven and earth, need to attune anew to the calling, the enabling, and the gifts of the Spirit of Christ. This would open us to the delightful interplay between God's initiative and calling, and our cooperation with the Spirit's leading and direction. God's desire for our world becomes our desire. God's work is what we seek to foster. It is stating the obvious that this is a mysterious rather than a predictable relationship. And it is dynamic. This interplay calls for discernment and great humility, as well as prayerfulness.

The purpose of this book is to explore responses both to the crises around us and the invitation of God at a time that may enable new ways to live the kingdom. The direction we have taken in the chapters that follow, is first to look to Jesus, and to his Sermon on the Mount. Prior to inviting people into his Beatitudes, we find Jesus at the center of suffering. We are told "people brought to Him all those who had various kinds of diseases, those in pain, those possessed by demons, those with epilepsy, and those who were paralyzed, and he healed them" (Matt 4:24 CEB). What Jesus will reveal to us today in the midst of the current pandemic, comes from the incarnation of God in the suffering of the world. Such incarnation will embrace the crucifixion, break the power of death through resurrection, and set free the joy and comforting presence of the Spirit to the end of the age. He invites our active participation.

Through his Beatitudes, Jesus offers his shape and character for our participation. Segundo Galilea suggests that "Jesus himself is the incarnation of the Beatitudes. Lived and proclaimed by Him, they become the spiritual values of a kingdom that is primarily Jesus himself."[1] The invitation for us is to embody and reflect these values as he does, and to renew our active and creative citizenship both of God's kingdom and of our troubled and suffering earthly realm. This is not a book about the Beatitudes as such, but rather it utilizes the Beatitudes as a framework. As empowering characteristics of kingdom life that, through the gift of the Spirit become part of Christ's indwelling presence, Jesus' Beatitudes give shape and substance to

1. Galilea, *The Way of Living Faith*, 49.

how we live and contextualize our kingdom, and earthly vocation in these new and challenging times.

In chapter 1 Christopher Brown identifies the Beatitudes as gifts of the Holy Spirit. He describes how the first Beatitude can help us acknowledge how times of crisis, anxiety, and change can bring us face to face with our poverty of spirit—the reminder that, despite what burdens weigh us down and trouble our souls, the realm of God's kingdom is wide open to us. The Holy Spirit calls, enables, and gifts us as guides to respond to troubled souls in this time of crisis. In Appendix 1 are reflection questions for this and the following chapters so that churches and home or book groups can discuss their responses, and so process the content and challenges of each chapter.

In chapter 2 Christopher Brown and Charles Ringma discuss how a time of crisis is a time of loss, even loss of illusions, and also fear of loss. This liminal space is a time to grieve, but also to find the comfort of the *One* who has suffered before us and now suffers with us. Loss may be the seedbed for a new receptivity both for the individual and for our church communities. At the end of chapter 2 is a meditation relating to being in liminal space, "Only the Lonely."

In chapter 3, Ross McKenzie, a scientist, argues that science begins with humility, an awareness of ignorance and a search for knowledge. He then reflects on what humility and meekness look like in science and daily life, humility before God, before others, and before nature. Humility, he says, is the noble choice to forgo your status, deploy your resources or use your influence for the good of others before yourself. He concludes that indeed the meek shall inherit the earth. A liturgy reflecting on our vulnerability concludes the chapter.

In chapter 4, Irene Alexander investigates the notion that the way of Jesus is the way of vulnerability. Fundamentally, that the image of Jesus on the cross is the image of the vulnerable God we are called to follow. Hungering and thirsting for righteousness will necessitate living out this vulnerable way, a vulnerability that extends to relationship with God, with the other, and with the earth. A liturgy reflecting on our vulnerability concludes the chapter.

In chapter 5, Tim McCowan explores the invitation to participate in God's mercy for persons and events in our world through the practice of intercessory prayer. To come face to face with a crisis, whether a person suffering a terrible illness, or a global community in the grip of a pandemic, confronts us with our vulnerability as humans. This chapter discusses how our experiences of powerlessness can be God's invitation into a deeper and more spacious encounter with God's mercy, presence, and power that can be shared with others as well as ourselves.

In chapter 6, Paul Mercer interweaves snippets of his life as a medical practitioner with his reflections on Scripture, and deals with his probing question: how to live in purity of heart. He explores the eight deadly thoughts as well as our responses of practices, participation, and productivity. The chapter concludes with a liturgy around being pure in heart.

Chapter 7 focuses on how we can support each other in times of crisis. Christopher Brown uses the context of a men's group where "Bob," who has lost his job as a result of the pandemic, now feels totally bereft. The interaction of the group demonstrates how we can become peacemakers by listening deeply, and trusting God's presence rather than fixing or giving advice.

In chapter 8 Charles Ringma demonstrates that the church, in its 2,000-year journey, has always had to face difficulties: some internal, such as doctrinal splits, misuse of power, and internal spiritual decay; but others such as wars, famines, pandemics, natural disasters, persecutions. The church has made various responses in these times of difficulty and the chapter contains some of the wisdom of the church's positive and creative responses, as well as the call to lament.

Chapter 9 is a conversation between Terry Gatfield and his friend Benson, an "economics guru," helping us understand the so-called dismal science of economics. Benson and the author also discuss some Christian perspectives on the economy and our place in it. This is important in the economic realities which take a hit in times of crisis.

Chapter 10 brings a majority world voice with biblical scholar Athena Gorospe writing about lament and liminality when disaster strikes. She uses Mark 13, the "Little Apocalypse," as well as Old Testament stories to explore responses to crises. The chapter concludes with a vigil for the voiceless.

In chapter 11, Sarah Nicholl likens the contemplation of God and the kingdom to Lucy's journey through the wardrobe to Narnia to meet Aslan. This journey beckons us to live both the promises of God's Beatitudes and the eschaton through the power of the Holy Spirit as Christian hope, in the expectation that God will bring transformation through this time of crisis, both in us and in our nations.

Interspersed between the chapters, we have included liturgies and prayers that may be used in church, home groups, online gatherings, or individually. These interludes remind us that to be a people of prayer, we need to pray. The prayer liturgy after chapter 10 is designed as a vigil, a time for being present with those who are suffering. While this outlines a long vigil, shorter sections may be used separately. The book concludes with additional prayers that can be prayed in times of crisis. In addition, as noted, we have included an appendix with questions designed for small group discussion, as well as an appendix outlining resources for further reading.

Finally, several of the chapters offer practices that can contribute to our readiness to participate in the life of the kingdom before, during, and after times of crisis. They prepare the way for the invitation to enter into and embody the beatitudinal life of Jesus. His life and teaching become thick and rich, and hold life-giving power for us and those around us, because of his life, crucifixion, resurrection, and abiding presence (Matt 1:23). Our living teacher is "with us to the end of this present age" (Matt 28:20 CEB). Our participation is commissioned by Jesus, who as our resurrected and ascended Lord, promises to be with us, leaving us with the unspoken life of the Spirit poured into our lives. It is the Spirit who mediates the joy of living the Beatitudes. Paul described our participation very clearly in this way: "Thus, I myself no longer live, but the Messiah lives in me, and the life I do now live in the flesh, I live by means of the faithfulness of the Son of God, who loved me by giving himself for me"(Gal 2:20).[2]

2. Translation by Michael J. Gorman, *Participating in Christ*, 117.

Blessed are the poor in spirit,
for theirs is the kingdom of heaven.

Lord, you always welcome our troubled souls,
and especially when we are at the end of our rope.
Your delight is to form us into the likeness of Jesus,
and though we are poor in spirit,
you refashion us as citizens of your kingdom.
Despite what burdens us,
you call us blessed and open to us your spacious
and generous kingdom realm.

1

Welcoming Troubled Souls

Christopher Brown

We join with you, our *reader*, in the context of a crisis, of a shared threat to our humanity. We might be likened to a youthful David, facing off the giant Goliath, armed with only five pebbles and a sling. How do we battle a contemporary giant, whose death-making and destructive footprints are enormous but, as a virus, is one thousand times smaller than a pinhead? David had no more than five pebbles and a sling. Invisible with him, and now amid our battles, is *One* who suffers the extremities of our crisis and comes alongside in response to our deepest heart-cries.

In this chapter, we consider how times of crisis can potentially hold up a mirror to the people we are. It can assist us to engage in sobering analysis, critique, and resolution. By contrast, a mirror held by the Holy Spirit might reveal to us our poverty of spirit and invite us into an encounter with God that is redemptive, spacious, and invitational. The Spirit's mirror may also reflect the changing shape of our character and actions as citizens of God's kingdom here on our troubled earth. In resourcing and reshaping us to journey through and beyond this time of global upheaval, the Spirit draws us back to Jesus' Sermon on the Mount, and gifts us anew with his eight life-giving and life-enhancing Beatitudes. Prayerfully attuning the ears and eyes of our hearts to the Spirit's whispers and prompts through these gifts, we will hear anew Jesus' invitation to live God's kingdom and become God's holy sanctuary here, in this world in crisis, and beyond.

God is Present

Though the shape of our dis-ease, anxieties, losses, and griefs differ, as do our daily circumstances, we all face the same adversary with meager resources. Perhaps no more than a sling and a few pebbles! And yet, you are also here, *Invisible One*! You come alongside in response to the deepest cry of each human heart and the groan of every troubled soul. What you, O God, face in all its totality during this time, would overwhelm us and throw us into despair. And yet, you take upon yourself all dimensions of this human suffering—every heart-cry, every groan, every fear, every death, every grief, forming no immunity to its potency and darkness! Your creation, O Spirit of God, matters. To you, our bodies matter, our flesh matters, our hearts matter, our consciousness matters, our death matters, as does our hope of your healing, restoration, and shalom. Taking our humanity upon yourself in this time of crisis, O Christ, with sacrificial self-giving, self-emptying, and receiving love of your Holy Trinity, you redeem our brokenness, reconcile us to God, and transform us into your likeness.

Whatever the footprints or carnage of the giants, you exceed their destructiveness through your offer of eternal life to be lived in the now as a miracle of incompleteness but future fulfillment. Encountering our troubled souls when at the end of our ropes, you readily refashion our disparate character into the likeness of Jesus and so shape our earthly habitation to embody our citizenship of your kingdom. Your eight *Beatitudinal* gifts, tailor-made for each of us, and edified by the words and messianic life of Jesus, re-form and animate us for such purpose. With the first gift, you engage with our troubled souls and our *poverty of spirit*. Despite what burdens weigh us down, you call us blessed and open to us the kingdom realm of God. In the spaciousness and safety of your enfolding, you hand us a second *gift*. With this, you encourage us to acknowledge our losses. Included are things we have held dear, as well as our shadowy parts, poor attachments, and illusions, which this time of crisis may have amplified and unmasked. You offer your comfort as we grieve and lament such losses.

Your invitations, *Invisible One*, to such vulnerabilities do not end here. With more *Beatitudinal gifts*, you empower us to grow in the gentle kingdom qualities of humility and kingdom-heartedness. You place within us a renewed hunger and thirst for God's reign of righteousness and justice here on earth, right amid our upheavals. You redeem and purify our hearts, fill them with your mercy, and invite us to be agents of your peace. You then animate within us the courage, and the caliber we need to have and be in order to experience persecution and opposition for your sake and the sake of your kingdom (Matt 5:3–10). *Invisible One*, you freely offer these eight *Beatitudinal gifts* and place them both before us, and within us.

Attempts to express the invitation of Jesus' beatitudes bring us to the edge of mystery. Here is a way of life to follow. At the same time, the Beatitudes shape the newness of life the Spirit has planted within us to be lived *in union* with Christ.

Crises, Mirrors, and Gifts

A time of crisis such as a pandemic, as previously indicated, can hold up the mirror as *to who we really are*.[1] We see more clearly the fragility and deficits of the institutions upon which we depend for our livelihoods, well-being, security, status, and control. Social commentators highlight deficits and pundits speculate on the shape of the interim and post-pandemic worlds. Given the material and racial axis upon which our societies turn, many are suffering far more than others—human collateral mirrored against prosperity, albeit with hints of anxiety! Some social analysis can be critical, confronting, contested, and competitive, especially where sectional interests are involved.

Will such mirrors be perspicacious enough to reflect the more intensely personal dimensions of *who we really are*? The etiology of the virus is of vital importance to researchers. What of the etiology of our disquiet, distress, disorientation, dread, or despair? A psychologically oriented mirror would focus on resourcing people to endure their anxiety, suffering, and sorrow until the crisis ends. Such an emphasis on coping is necessary. And yet, what if the mirror tilts towards the soul? Christine Jeske suggests that the orientation of biblical prophets, who walked with people through catastrophes, was beyond mere endurance. Their focus was on "proactively changing relationships with each other and with God."[2] The prophetic mirror, which is able to reflect the soul, would light upon an alternative etiology to our ills. It could bring into sharper relief the dual nature of our citizenship. The hand which holds such a mirror could embrace our human vulnerabilities and take the pulse of our souls!

Holding such a mirror, the Holy Spirit reveals how our human vulnerabilities are indeed embraced within the sacrificial, self-giving, self-emptying, and gracious-receiving love of the Holy Trinity. The Spirit's gentle invitations

1. Frank M. Snowden, cited in Chotiner, "How Pandemics Change History."
2. Jeske, "This Pandemic Hits Americans Where We're Spiritually Weak."

for our souls come amid our disquiet, distress, disorientation, dread, or despair. Our soul, even in its shyness, can be coaxed closer to the edge of this mystery. The soul's receptive ear becomes attuned to the Spirit's whispers and prompts. It is the Holy Spirit as Paraclete who comes alongside in response to the deepest cries and groaning of our hearts (Rom 8:26). Psalmic utterances indicate that the disquiet, disturbance, and downcast state of the soul, reveal an intrinsic yearning for the Living God (Ps 43:5).

Blessed are the Poor in Spirit

With the Paraclete alongside us, and in the safety and spaciousness of the intimate relationship with Christ through the Spirit, we are encouraged to open our hands to receive the Spirit's first *Beatitudinal gift*: "Blessed are the poor in spirit, for theirs is the kingdom of heaven" (Matt 5:3). The changing circumstances brought by the pandemic test our human capacities, often mirroring at a deeper level who we really are. Jesus engages us in our unworthiness, our inadequacy, our failings, our faint-heartedness, and where we are overwhelmed and impotent in the face of the giant imprint of COVID-19. Jesus meets us, as we do those around us, in our poverty of spirit; an inner and outer poverty which, in his presence, amplifies the need for something—Someone—far greater than ourselves. At the point at which our need for God is greatest, Jesus opens wide the doorway to kingdom citizenship and invites our participation in his life and purposes here on earth. In this way, his kingdom will become incarnated in our troubled world.

It is our poverty of spirit that we bring into this relational intimacy with Jesus. We might think of this *Beatitudinal gift* as a gathering place—a place of encounter—in which all that burdens and distresses us is welcomed, including all that troubles our minds, induces fear, and erodes our confidence, especially all that is prompted by the pandemic. Being awakened to such poverty brings us face to face with our absolute need for God. Though pastoral guides and spiritual companions can help in extending the welcome of Jesus, the Spirit, who is the Spirit of Christ, is our primary and constant guide.

Imagine the gentle encounter that might occur between the Spirit and our awakened and receptive soul as we hold this *Beatitudinal gift*.

> What is it, *dear soul*, that so burdens and distresses you,
> troubles your mind, heightens your anxieties,
> induces fear, and erodes your confidence?

How is it you feel so exposed and naked?
Have those illusions of seeking what does not satisfy,
of finding distraction, or of filling empty spaces,
begun to fall away?

What of those cracks in the identity?
you have cobbled together,
as you sought to make your own way
and to be as self-reliant as possible?

What of the niggles of guilt and flushes of shame?
that have bubbled to the surface,
as you began to see more of who you are;
including those that initially made you angry,
so that your first response was to blame others?

What of your disquiet, *dear soul*?
Are you noticing something deep within?
you may have pushed aside, neglected,
or with which you have not kept faith?

Why, *o soul*, do you perceive God as so distant,
engage in self-condemnation,
and consider yourself as unworthy,
as if a bottomless void has opened between you?

Such encounters between the Spirit and the awakened and receptive soul would rarely involve interrogation. Rather than judgments, they are the stirrings, whispers, and noticings of *love*. When the soul encounters the Spirit, the language may be more that of poetry (such as in the Psalms), metaphor, imagery, or parable-like story. When pastoral guides attune to the promptings of the Spirit, they can assist troubled pilgrims to discern these inner stirrings and disturbances as entryways deeper into the soul. In the divine embrace, pilgrims can be awakened to the poverty of self-reliance and discover that the deepest yearnings of their souls are for intimacy with God. The realm of God's kingdom opens wide to welcome them.

The Spirit engages with our humanity at its rawest edge. An alcoholic, in the Twelve Step Recovery, would tell us that! At the end of his rope and realizing he is thoroughly beat; he lifts the head he was cradling in the gutter to cry out for the help of his "Higher Power." Then in recovery, he would acknowledge that only God could "put the cork in my bottle!" So little left of him; so much of God! Is it strange that the gutter ushers us into the threshold of the house of the Lord? And so it is with such graciousness, Jesus can say how happy and blessed we are in being poor in spirit, for ours is the kingdom of heaven (Matt 5:3). It is the breath of God that stirs our hearts.

Breath of God

O breath of God, you stir our hearts
We're weary with longing for you
Come raise our dead, mend every breach
We're weary with longing for you.

Restore all things, remove the veil
We're watching with longing for you
We take this bread, we drink this cup
We're watching with longing for you. (Tom Wuest)[3]

Pastoral Responders

How might pastoral guides respond during a time when personal and societal upheaval amplifies the poverty of our human predicament, when crisis becomes a catalyst for change, and when the breath of the Spirit stirs up profound longings deep within our souls? Such guides need to be closely attuned to the whispers and prompts of the Spirit as they welcome troubled souls. In turn, they will encourage pilgrims to also attend to what the breath of God is stirring in their hearts. It is the Spirit who calls, forms, and shapes pastoral guides for such tasks. The Spirit places within them the open-arm welcome of Jesus' "Come to me," along with his gentle and humble heart. Inwardly resourced and animated in such a manner, guides can enable pilgrims to bring their anxious and burdened hearts into relational intimacy with Jesus (Matt 11:28–30).

Personal and Prophetic

The call of the Spirit on pastoral responders is both personal and prophetic, especially during these troubled times. Christine Jeske suggests the biblical prophets not only assisted people to endure the crisis, but to proactively seek

3. Wuest, "Breath of God."

changed relationships, one with another, and with God.[4] Significant change most often begins at a profoundly personal level. Guides have a role in assisting pilgrims to bring the stirrings of their troubled heart and the longings of their souls into a "condition of disclosure and discovery." This may be "almost the greatest service that any human being ever performs for another."[5] This needs to occur in tandem with the Spirit—the Paraclete—who comes alongside to answer the deepest heart-cry. This unique partnership can open a safe, spacious, non-judgmental, and sacred space in which the troubled soul can emerge. The revelation that the soul flourishes in God can lead to the unfolding of the character and dynamic of the *Beatitudinal gifts*, which are both personal and prophetic. We can mourn with those who mourn, humbly engage in kingdom-heartedness, thirst for justice and God's right way of living, extend mercy, have uncluttered hearts and clarity of sight, become peacemakers, and find fortitude in the face of opposition.

An illustration of a soul-oriented encounter is provided in chapter 7, under the title of "Guides for the Soul." The pilgrim, whom I call Bob, has been impacted by the pandemic crisis and is offered guidance and support in a small faith-based group setting. The guide, Joe, opens a welcoming group space, listens prayerfully and attentively to Bob, discerns the Spirit's prompts, and notices the points of entry into the deeper regions of Bob's soul. Group members form with Bob the solidarity of Christ's presence and offer a prayerful holding for this encounter. They know that they, too, are poor in spirit and in much need of God.

Crisis and Change

The Spirit invites our participation in such life-giving and life-enhancing responses in times of crisis. As we are gathered into Christ by the Spirit, Jesus' *Beatitudes* and his cruciform life can form our character as citizens of God's kingdom lived out as God's citizens here on earth. The mirror held by the Spirit reflects our poverty of spirit through a high optic lens—the lens of the cross! Our crisis, though it might signal danger, becomes a catalyst for significant change. The soul can stir within a troubled frame! It can open up for discovery, disclosure, and the renewal of life and faith. Having offered intimate accompaniment through the pandemic and engaged us in our poverty of spirit, the Spirit may seek tiny cracks in our

4. Jeske, "This Pandemic Hits Americans Where We're Spiritually Weak."

5. Steere, *Gleanings*, 83.

resistances through which to gain entry. One wonders if the uncontainable and life-giving Spirit is opportunistic!

With the Spirit's calling, accompaniment, and animation, we embody and reflect Jesus' way of walking through crises with troubled souls. With the pandemic crisis, triggering societal upheavals that reverberate in the human heart, the call comes for God's people of praise and participation to renew their desire to live God's kingdom and become God's holy sanctuary here on earth (Ps 114:2). Descriptive words fail us, so we move to prayer to express our gratitude for such freely given and transforming gifts.

Lord,
You became poor to meet us amid our poverty,
opening to us your kingdom realm, and
drawing us into the community of the *persons* of the Trinity.

As you grieved so profoundly over Jerusalem,
and took upon your person the sins and sufferings of our world,
you stand in solidarity with us
as we mourn over our world in this time of global crisis.

Being one with us in our poverty and our grieving,
you invite us to participate in your dying,
and to be raised with you in newest of life,
as the Spirit reshapes us in your kingdom-heartedness,
meekness, and humility.

Your Spirit stirs within our spirits your passion,
your hunger and thirst for right and just kingdom living,
renewing us to embody the character
of your kingdom citizenship.

The Spirit gifts us with your indwelling presence,
and invites our full participation in your life and purposes
in our crisis-plagued world.
It is through your grace we are enabled to express your tender mercies,
your way of peace, and establish your solidarity
with troubled souls.

From the purity of your uncluttered and humble heart,
you open the eyes of our hearts to glimpse God's presence and actions
within us and in the world around us.

You provide your courage, caliber, and protective presence
when we experience opposition and persecution,
as did you for your prophets of old.

Lord,
Amid this crisis,
you open the door to your kingdom,
encouraging us to seek here on earth
what is in heaven.

We experience in you what we most long for
in the depths of our souls,
and find satisfaction, fruitfulness, mercy, and peace
as the Spirit renews our citizenship
of both heaven and earth.

We are indeed blessed, enlivened, and animated
and, despite our limitations, hesitations, and misgivings,
are enabled to participate joyfully
in the way of the Beatitudes,
in your life and purposes, during this time of crisis.

As the kingdom character and dynamics of your Beatitudes
unfold in and through us, shaping us in your likeness,
not only do we discover and join in your engagement in our world in crisis,
but you offer us glimpses of the world free of crisis
that is yet to come.
Amen.

Blessed are those who mourn,
for they will be comforted.

Lord, in the spaciousness and safety of your enfolding,
you encourage us to acknowledge our losses.
These include things we have held dear,
also our shadowy parts—poor attachments and illusions,
which have been unmasked in this time of crisis.
You offer your comfort as we grieve and lament these losses.
And you invite us to a place of receptivity and new life.

2

Mourning, Comfort, and the "New Normal"

Charles Ringma and Christopher Brown

Unfamiliar Territory

In the experience of crisis and upheaval, it is likely that most of us will suddenly find that life is no longer normal. Our usual routines and rhythms have disappeared, and we now find ourselves in unfamiliar territory. This goes to show how much we are creatures of habit and of regularity, and how uncomfortable we can become when sudden changes crash in upon us.

When these normal patterns of living suddenly change, and particularly when this is due to external factors, many feel that they have been thrown off their perch. Scholars call this entering into a liminal space. Liminality indicates the idea of being in unfamiliar territory and in an in-between space. The old has suddenly been interrupted, and the new is unclear and uncertain. While one may pine for the old and impatiently seek to grab the new, the liminal space invites us to something quite different. While this difference may well involve impatience and frustration, the challenge is to embrace the stance of creative waiting. And in this waiting the most productive impulse is: what can I learn here, what may need to change, and what new things or patterns of living need to emerge? Thus, liminality is akin to pregnancy or being in a womb-like state. This notion can also be considered as part of the cruciform nature of the kingdom of God, where the death of the old "normal" takes place as one is raised in Christ to new life. In this chapter, where we explore dimensions of liminality, we might speak of a "womb of mourning, comfort, and transformation," as we seek the renewal of the kingdom in our earthly citizenship and in our faith communities in this in-between and crisis-impacted space.

One positive and challenging move in all of this is to become more self-reflective. The well-known Australian journalist Paul Kelly has made the point that the cultivation of a strong inner life is essential at this time of crisis with COVID-19. He goes on to note that this has certainly not been a preoccupation of contemporary culture. And ends with the probing question: "do people [still] know what an inner life means?"[1]

Such a question can and should be posed by people of faith. Can we become more prayerfully self-reflective in this time of crisis? This is quite different than mere self-preoccupation—for in this, we are merely on our own. But inward affinity with Christ offers depth and a rich dynamic for such inner exploration, since we are not on our own, but with the One who loves us and gave his life for us. It is the Spirit of Christ who stands with us amid our crisis. It is he who takes on our pains and sufferings in redeeming, reconciling, and transformative ways. A life crisis, therefore, can be the catalyst that reorients us towards the soulful dimensions of our citizenship, both in heaven and earth. In chapter 7, we will briefly meet Bob, who through crisis, was on the cusp of being helped to engage in such self-reflection. In the context of social upheaval, insecurity, and suffering, the challenge and encouragement are to remain attentive to our pain and grief. The challenge is also to find an inner solidarity with the calamities and losses of people in the world around us. This is the encouragement of the second Beatitude.

Mourning Our Losses

The second Beatitude of mourning, comfort, and eventual transformation opens an inner space for prayerful reflection and grieving over our calamities and losses and those of others. There can be a loss of what we have held dear, including hopes and dreams and long-term securities. Crisis as a catalyst may have unmasked things we have only entertained in the shadows, including less than life-giving attachments, illusions, and even addictions. At worst, there may have been the loss of loved ones. Then there is the loss of certainty in being unhoused from our normal ways of life and experiencing the liminal, or in-between spaces, without clarity regarding the future. There

1. Kelly, "Coronavirus."

is loss and suffering both within and without! This Beatitude is one for the womb-like state of liminality. Through it, Jesus invites us to stand amid such losses, pain, suffering and even despair, to mourn, to grieve, and to lament, and to be as attentive to our interior life as we seek to be in the world around us. This involves facing human loss, suffering, frailty, and mortality with humility and courage. It can be an opportunity to acknowledge our experience of abandonment, and even to express our angst and our questions of "why me?" and "how long, O Lord?" And we should do this even if initially these questions seem only to echo in dark voids.

In the early stages of mourning, our eyes may be too dimmed with tears, our spirits too sore, and the ears of our heart too deafened by the inner vocalization of our pressing needs. And thus we fail to notice the One who has come alongside of us. It is the Spirit who attunes to our deepest heart-cry and offers divine reciprocity in our sufferings and longings. The Spirit knows and identifies with those emotional sighs and groans that are too deep for words. All this is known to God, as are the Spirit's heartfelt desires for us. It is the Spirit as our passionate advocate who pleads for us—the children and citizens of God's kingdom—before God the Father. Rather than an anxious retreat into the residues of the old normal, or to scramble blindly to fashion the new, the second Beatitude encourages us to wait for the inner movement of the Spirit who has come alongside bringing comfort in response to our deepest heart-cry. We mourn, grieve, and lament in relational reciprocity and in the depths of our humanity, but where we are fully known by the Loving Other. In these interior spaces vacated through loss, the Spirit cultivates an inner spaciousness from which new and abundant life can flow. It is here we encounter the suffering and crucified Christ. The womb of liminality becomes a holy womb!

The "Suffering One"

The second Beatitude involves our participation with the suffering and crucified Christ. Should we fall into despair and forsakenness, the Spirit holds for us the hope of resurrection and new life. It is in our poverty of spirit, in the extremities of our human frailty and vulnerability, in our grief and our lament, that we are fully known. Every dimension of our lives is continually woven together in Christ, being transformed into his likeness to mesh with God's kingdom plan for us (Rom 8:26–29). The comfort of this Beatitude is that we mourn in the presence of our God, who is our refuge and the sustainer of our lives.

It is not the acceptance of sufferance per se, or our endurance, fortitude, and self-denial that is edifying, but rather our mourning in the redeeming, reconciling, transforming presence of the Spirit. We are invited to consecrate by faith not only our pain and suffering, but our whole person. We yield the whole of ourselves in our distress. Suffering opens to us the depth of our poverty of spirit and to what is profoundly personal. At its most intense, our pain is almost incommunicable, and sorely tests the adequacy of human compassion, leaving us most alone. Perhaps one of the most potent public cries amid the pandemic has been of people dying alone. Without God's presence, grace, and abundant mercy, our humanity is lost!

In the divine comfort and blessing of our mourning, we can express the very depths of who we are, what we have desired to be, and what in the experience of grace we are becoming—contradictions and all.[2] In the consecration of our pain and suffering in faith and in God's abundant mercy, we are marked primarily by our citizenship of God's kingdom and a new identity is given as we die and rise with Christ who gathers all the sufferings of our life. As Thomas Merton concludes: "Suffering should call out our name and the name of Christ."[3]

This call to turn inward is most appropriate not only because of the changed circumstances, but also because this is something we have neglected in the more ordinary realities of life where we are busy, distracted, preoccupied, and non-reflective. In the renewal of our citizenship, we discover that the womb of mourning, comfort, and transformation is a holy womb that births transformation. Far more of us is required than one minute of mindfulness that does little to ground and orient us. Far from encouraging selfish self-centeredness, reflection reorients us in the way of Christ to others, to the life around us, and toward God, as renewed citizens of God's heavenly and earthly kingdoms.

A Crisis of Limitation

Amongst the many social impacts of the pandemic crisis, are the constrictions placed on everyday life. Despite the uncertainty concerning periods of lockdown and social distancing, commentators have begun to speculate

2. Merton, *No Man is an Island*, 84–85.

3. Merton, *No Man is an Island*, 85.

about a new normal with little specificity as to what new things or patterns might emerge. The notion of liminality, mentioned earlier, might be expressed as moving from a familiar and long occupied house, onto life on the road, and not quite knowing where the next dwelling is or how it might look. As we step out onto the path, a mist surrounds us, enveloping the way ahead. These constrictions of our everyday life can bring us face to face with what has been called a crisis of limitation. How then might the misty, womb-like state of liminality become a holy and transformative womb?

Here is the personal account of one of our authors, Charles Ringma, reflecting on "sameness":

With the lockdown I was first rather happy. Being an introvert, I was happy to be at home and felt I had more time than usual to get on with research and writing, although I did miss going to the library. However, as time went on, several things began to happen. The first was too much of a focus on the pandemic. And since I come from the Netherlands and have lived and worked in Asia and in Canada, I was constantly looking at what was happening in these countries, as well as developments in Australia. Secondly, I was beginning to feel despondent, particularly when certain countries seemed to make such inadequate responses to the crisis. Thirdly, I have become increasingly concerned as to what will happen in a post-coronavirus world. Will things go back to normal? Or will there be significant changes in our world? And finally, I have been impacted by a sense of boredom. Every day seems so much like the day before. And tomorrow the day will probably be like today.

As this mist began to lift, I glimpsed a little of monasticism! If there is anything true about the monastic community, it is the "sameness" and regularity of each day. As a consequence, monks have had to come to terms with the problem of *acedia*. Simply put, this Greek term means apathy/boredom/torpor. More deeply, it means "absence of care," and a person "afflicted by acedia refuses to care or is incapable of doing so."[4] This was called dealing with the "noonday demon," because the heartbeat of monastic life is the opposite of acedia. It is attentiveness to God, one's inner being, the community, and concern for the wider world. Acedia was seen as a temptation.

(See Appendix 2 for resources on the Christian faith tradition.)

4. Norris, *Acedia & Me*, 3.

The Challenge of "Sameness"

In light of my understanding of acedia, I am having problems with "sameness." And this is not surprising since life in the modern world is about the opposite. It is about distraction, diversity, travel, and living with multiple options. When this is no longer possible, it is understandable that one may become frustrated and even depressed. Thus, the mental health impacts of the coronavirus are very real for this and many other reasons.

I would encourage you, the reader, to reflect on how you are dealing with the "noonday demon." What I am trying to do is to embrace a practical asceticism. I don't need travel, holidays, or a night at the movies in order to be at peace and to live with gratitude. I can be thankful for what *this* day brings, even if it is much the same as yesterday. Moreover, I need to avoid seeking distraction to feel okay. Distraction cannot possibly meet my needs anyway. And finally, I need to wrestle with my most basic need—why am I not at peace with what God gives me in this "ordinary" day? That is my challenge! Such a challenge can be part of our renewal of citizenship in the earthly kingdom which, as suggested above, is so often about distraction, diversity, travel, and living with multiple options.

Losses on a Societal Level

In the first part of this chapter, the focus was on personal losses. At a societal level, much has also been lost—jobs, businesses, homes, general health and well-being. More than that, our economies have received such a blow that recovery will take many years, if not decades. And who knows what else will be lost in the aftermath of COVID-19. Possible more profound losses may include the loss of confidence in our global order, in our governments, and in other social institutions. And some may be entertaining doubts about the future of the church and other religious associations.

In countries that have not been so severely impacted by this pandemic, the refrain is *back to normal as soon as safely possible.* And while this is understandable, we hope that this time of abnormality has taught us something so that there will be a *new* normal that we all aspire to and will work towards.

We believe that the hope for a new normal is also appropriate for the church. We hope that the present-day church won't rush back to the old normal. Such a rush would miss the invitation of the second Beatitude.

Acknowledgment of this time of liminality is vital for the church, as the womb of mourning, comfort, and transformation. This is especially so because the church of the old normal has been far too captive to the dominant ethos of contemporary culture, and has functioned too much on a business model for its institutional life. Moreover, the church has hardly exemplified its communal identity in Christ through the Spirit, and has failed to function as a prophetic community in society.

Thus, this time of loss, shut-down, and liminality is a time that needs to be welcomed and preserved for as long as necessary. As church we should neither simply pine for the old ways, nor should we jump into the future with premature solutions. Instead, we need to wait. Liminality is a sabbath gift. And as the womb of the Spirit, we need the pregnancy to go the full distance. And in waiting we may well need to come first and foremost not to the new normal, but to repentance and transformation regarding the idolatries of the past.

Loss and Asceticism

It is hard to predict what a new normal may look like for the renewal of kingdom citizenship and for the church, but one lesson that can be drawn from our present circumstances is learning from the present realities of *loss.* Rather than seeing loss as an enemy, we may learn to see it as friend. And loss is a companion to emptiness, and emptiness may be the seedbed for a new receptivity.

Of course, it is right that we have emphasized the blessings that we receive in the Christian life. We have gained much through Christ's redemptive love, even life itself. And in Christ, we have gained as gift the life-giving Spirit. But we have failed to accent the reality of loss. And loss brings us into the domain of asceticism, which from the Greek, *asketikos,* means sacrifice for the purpose of training and formation (as in a sport). And by way of application, sacrifice, and self-discipline, for the sake of growing in Christlikeness and service.

Asceticism has not always had a good track record in Christian spirituality. At times, ascetic practices have negated the body, made salvation a self-effort, and reflected a distorted view of God. Bradley Holt rightly notes that a faulty asceticism "leads to despising God's good gifts of creation: our bodies and the world around us."[5]

5. Holt, *Thirsty for God*, 38.

However, there have also been laudable perspectives and practices. While in religious orders and the priesthood, the dominant commitments have been poverty, celibacy, and obedience, for the laity ascetic practices have traditionally included prayer, fasting and almsgiving, and acts of generosity.

But all of this can be framed much more basically. Asceticism is far more central to the Christian life than merely fasting. Coming to faith in Christ involves the loss of the old life of human autonomy and self-sufficiency, and embracing the new life in Christ. In coming to Christ, we hand over to him our sin *and* our goodness, in fact, our very selves. And this new life involves a life of obedience and openness to the Spirit. Thus, it involves the loss of going our way and a life of self-sufficiency.

There is also more that we need to surrender. The love of God involves us in a commitment to seeing God's shalom erupt into our world, and the love of neighbor involves us in service to the other. What this means practically is that we are willing to lay things aside and to sacrifice so that a something much better can swim into view. In the light of these perspectives, it should be clear that ascetic practices lie at the very heart of Christian spirituality, service, and kingdom citizenship.

So the question for us in this time of COVID-19, when we have already experienced so much loss, is: *what is it that we need to learn in anticipating the new normal about living more prayerfully and sacrificially?* In other words, do we need to become more ascetic? Do we need to embrace loss in new and productive ways? Is the desert as important as the promised land? Is "not-having" as important as having?

In taking these questions on board, we may need to hear the challenge of St. John Chrysostom: "Those who live in the world, even though married, ought to resemble the monks in everything else."[6] Clearly, Chrysostom is making the point that there should not be a huge difference between monks and the laity. Ordinary Christians also need to live in community, practice hospitality, live prudently, live in obedience to the gospel, and live in fidelity. Thus, like the monks, we too need to practice asceticism and in relinquishing the good, we make way for the greater good in the kingdom of God.

6. Ringma, *Hear the Ancient Wisdom*, 14.

Provisionality of Earthly Life

A crisis can reveal to us the provisionality of our human existence. The scale in terms of infections and death of the pandemic brings us face to face with our mortality. Questions are also asked about the sovereignty of God. Have we in the Western world focused too much attention on blessing and much-having, with God as the perennial giver? Has this one-sided notion of God's relationship with us been somewhat dinted in this time of pandemic? What most people are now grappling with is not the reality of blessing, but the challenges of pain and struggle amid *loss*.

Might our notion of liminality as a womb-like state help us here? Does the crisis of limitation reflect a greater magnitude? Like stepping into the mist, as mentioned above, we only partially see the sovereignty of God in the present world, in the church, and in our personal lives, for we are living between the times (1 Cor 13:12). We look for solutions and finality concerning the pandemic, but live in the tension of not knowing fully. Can this also be a reminder that God's actions in this world and with us as his people has no immediate grand finality to it?[7] It is full of tension and it is marked by provisionality. A significant perspective on God's sovereignty in such a time is that of the eschaton, God's final future (1 Cor 15:24–26). But in the meantime, "God's rulership is being advanced and expanded by the work of the Holy Spirit in the world."[8]

The same is true of the New Testament, even regarding the coming of Christ. This is most basically illustrated by "the yet" and the "not-yet" nature of the kingdom of God. As G. E. Ladd notes, "the church lives 'between the times'; the old age goes on, but the powers of the new age have irrupted into the old age." He goes on to further illustrate the creative tensions here. "The church," he notes, "is the people of the kingdom, never that kingdom itself," but the "kingdom creates the church, works through the church, and is proclaimed in the world by the church."[9] Is the kingdom, in our era of crisis, in our liminality, the holy womb?

In the midst our mourning, our grieving, and lamenting, it can be hard to connect our sufferings and pain to the larger narrative through which we make meaning of our lives. It can feel like a part of the story that we would like to skip over and for things to quickly return to what we know

7. Brueggemann, *Theology of the Old Testament*, 83.

8. Grenz, *Theology for the Community of God*, 107.

9. Ladd, *A Theology of the New Testament*, 69, 113, 119.

as normal. And yet, in this place of the divine presence, and of mourning, comfort, and transformation, we are invited to articulate our reality, feel our pain, and lament our losses. Just as in the provisional nature of our kingdom citizenship in the yet and the not-yet, and our living in the hope of God's final future, the second Beatitude encourages us as kingdom citizens and as communities of faith, not to get ahead of ourselves. To clamor too quickly beyond our liminality can be to miss the invitations of the Spirit, who takes hold of us in our human frailty to empower us in our weakness (Rom 8:26), offers comfort amid our losses, and embraces us in God's holy womb of mourning, comfort, and transformation.

In the following liturgy you are invited to prayer and meditation on loneliness and God's comfort.

"Only the Lonely": A Meditation

Paul Mercer

Give us Barabbas (the father's son), we shouted.

Jesus (the Son of the Father) was taken and whipped. Then he was alone.

Social isolation, shutdown, hard shutdown.

Lord, these new familiar words threaten all our relationships. They sanitize friendships. Before the time of crisis emerged, many in our world knew the relentless power of loneliness. Some adapted, some struggled on, while many suffered silently. "Look at all the lonely people," our singers sang.

Like Jesus, the lonely wept. [Silence]

Read: Job 24:1–12 Zephaniah 3:17 John 11:9, 27–36

Our world is the garden of your creative love. From the earth you shaped us and breathed life into our humanity. You made us with a "belongingness" that remembers your desire to walk with us in the cool of the evening; that remembers we belong to each other, "male and female," for mutual relationships, for cooperation, and loving our neighbor.

Lord, the whole world groans with this longing. In crisis, we see this in sheer relief. Beauty and decay mix to despair.

Like Jesus, we share the sweat of distress. [Silence]

Read: Psalm 4:6–8 Luke 22:39–46

Lord, why does loneliness diminish us? Why do we become deflated? The promise of your divine image within fades in "isolation." We lose confidence in ourselves. Social clumsiness replaces the joy of friendship. Our health declines. We stop exercising. We are frightened to go out into the world. In this time of pandemic, we have become sterile. We seek relief in the fermented fruit of the vine, in gaming machines and other substances. Our mental health and social functioning begin to fail.

Like Jesus lifted up, we pant for relief. [Silence]

Read: Psalm 22:1–5, 19–25 John 14:15–21

God said, "Let us make humanity in our image, to resemble us so that they may take charge of the fish of the sea, the birds of the sky, the livestock, all the earth and all crawling things on earth." With deep sadness, we acknowledge our many failings. Often, we the people of the earth have betrayed your earth-keeping trust. In countless ways we have turned our back on you and your calling. In self-interest, autonomy, and careless regard for our neighbors, we have often been hard-hearted. Our personal intensity has let trees fall, species die out, and this planet warm dangerously.

Lonely people are human collateral damage. Financial contingency, physical inactivity, downwardly spiraling self-worth sidelines the productivity of such people.

Lord, raise us up from the fog of our complacency. May the shocks of crisis bring us to our senses, and to repentance.

Like Jesus' faithful cross-shaped love, may we as the people of new creation, mandate creation-care. [Silence]

Read: Psalm 104:1–9, 24–31 1 Corinthians 1:4–9

"I'm so lonely I could cry." This lament pounds with the beat of our hearts.

Sweet Jesus, our master and friend until the end of the age, we call for you to be closer than a brother or sister for all who are alone. In crisis, we recognize that all of us carry a sense of being alone and afraid.

When minds are swirling or during long dark nights; when mental health is collapsing and choosing death seems inviting, remind us, and all who are lonely, that your love never ends. Your grace, peace, and healing are ever present to us. Give us the gift of good sleep. Moderate our irritability. Restrain violence, especially in our homes. Step from the shadows and embrace us with the communion of the Father, Son, and Spirit.

Like Jesus, first-born of the resurrected from the dead, give us hope that endures.

[Silence]

Read: Psalm 102:1–12 2 Corinthians 4:6–11

May all who are alone discover the comfort of being accepted, of being listened to. We say, "a problem shared is a problem halved." May we, constrained by the love of Jesus, bear each other's burdens. Refocus our eyes and ears to all who are alone. Fill all your people with your Spirit afresh so that in times of crisis we love all our neighbors, especially the lonely, as Christ loves us and gave himself for us. Holy Dove, our comforter, blow the freshness of Jesus' resurrection presence into the lives of all who struggle in crisis.

We are waiting for the dawn of your light, of new creation, of life eternal, to be with friends who come home rejoicing.

Dear Jesus, who humbly offers through faithful, self-giving love, to befriend and heal all who are burdened in times of crisis, be with us now. Transform our lives toward the hope of your glory.

[Silence]

Read: Psalm 91:1–7 Romans 15:13 Revelation 21:3–4

St Patrick's Breastplate

I arise today through
God's strength to pilot me, God's might to uphold me,
God's wisdom to guide me, God's eye to see before me,
God's ear to hear me, God's word to speak for me,
God's hand to guard me, God's way to lie before me,
God's shield to protect me, God's host to secure me—
against snares of devils,
against temptations and vices,
against inclinations of nature,
against everyone who shall wish me ill,
afar and anear,
alone and in a crowd . . .
Christ, be with me, Christ before me, Christ behind me,
Christ in me, Christ beneath me, Christ above me,
Christ on my right, Christ on my left, Christ where I lie, Christ where I sit,
Christ where I arise, Christ in the heart of everyone who thinks of me,
Christ in the mouth of everyone who speaks of me,
Christ in every eye that sees me, Christ in every ear that hears me.
Salvation is of the Lord.
Salvation is of the Lord.
Salvation is of the Christ.
May your salvation, O Lord, be ever with us.

Grace and peace to all.

Blessed are the meek,
for they will inherit the earth.

Lord, as we let go of, and grieve what we once held dear,
you empower us to grow in the gentle kingdom qualities
of humility and kingdom-heartedness,
where our identity and our vocation is found in you.
As we embrace humility before God, before each other and before nature,
we become your holy sanctuary, here on earth as it is in heaven,
and you invite us to become agents of your kingdom here amid our troubled world.

3

Blessed are the Meek

The Science and Theology of Humility

Ross H. McKenzie

A crisis is disorienting. Regardless of the origin or nature of the crisis it often leads to anxiety and questions, whether at the personal, institutional, or societal level. At all of these levels we operate with certain assumptions, values, expectations, worldviews, plans, and ambitions. Yet, these can be turned upside down or shredded by a crisis, no matter how powerful we are or how many resources we might have.

A Crisis Humbles

The USA is the wealthiest and most powerful nation on earth. It is at the forefront of medical research and has some of the best hospitals in the world. Yet, in May 2020, *The Economist* magazine reported: "Doctors and nurses at Northwell Health have treated nearly 40,000 Covid-19 cases, more than any other American provider. But Michael Dowling, who runs New York state's largest hospital firm, is not triumphant. 'This crisis has humbled us,' he sighs. The same goes for much of America's $4 trillion health-care sector."[1]

1. *The Economist*, "The pandemic will recast America's health-care industrial complex."

The US government spends more than 700 billion dollars each year on the military with the goal to protect its citizens and project its power all around the world. Yet, COVID-19 has brought the USA to its knees. An invisible virus particle, SARS-CoV2, a thousand times smaller than a pinhead, has reproduced and spread rapidly through the country. It has killed more than four hundred thousand people and led to the unemployment of millions. The death toll is far greater than the number of US citizens killed in the wars in Korea, Vietnam, Iraq, and Afghanistan combined. How the mighty are fallen! Yet tragically, such a fall is not new. For example, it also happened to the Roman Empire. In his seminal book *Rats, Lice, and History*, Hans Zinsser notes that "again and again, the forward march of Roman power and world organization, was interrupted by the only force against which political genius and military valor were utterly helpless: epidemic disease . . . And when it came as though carried on storm clouds, all other things gave way, and men crouched in terror, abandoning all their quarrels, undertakings, and ambitions, until the tempest had blown over."[2]

A crisis such as the COVID-19 pandemic illustrates some truths that we struggle to accept, particularly in the affluent Western world:

> *We have limited control over our destinies.*
>
> *We are interconnected at the relational, economic, political, and biological level.*
>
> *We have a common humanity that transcends race, class, wealth, power, age, religion, and citizenship.*
>
> *We cannot see certain realities.*
>
> *We need to listen to others, including experts and those with different backgrounds and perspectives than us.*
>
> *Science and technology do not have all the answers to the major challenges of today.*

These uncomfortable truths need to be wrestled with at the individual, institutional, and social level. I will reflect on how a common element in our response should be humility. Indeed, blessed are the meek!

2. Quoted in Stark, *The Rise of Christianity*, 74.

Science Begins and Ends in Humility

Science requires humility. Any scientific investigation starts with acknowledging ignorance. Scientific progress requires a willingness to admit mistakes and accept evidence, even when it goes against cherished and esteemed beliefs, theories, and colleagues.

As a scientist I am fascinated by the science of COVID-19, from the genetic code of the virus to the mathematical modeling of epidemics. I find it amazing how much we do know. It is also amazing how much we do *not* know.

The SARS-CoV2 virus is one of many coronaviruses, a name derived from the crown-like appearance of a virus particle in an electron microscope. The points on the crown are called spike proteins. They are attached to a spherical surface composed of other proteins. The diameter of the virus particle is about one-tenth of a micron. If you lined up 10,000 particles next to each other in a straight line, they would be the size of a pinhead. The complete details of the atomic composition and geometrical arrangement of these spike proteins has been determined. This sphere (virus capsid) encapsulates the genetic information that is encoded in a single strand of an RNA molecule. The spike proteins allow a virus particle to attach itself to and enter a human respiratory cell. Inside the cell the virus particle bursts, releasing the RNA molecule that then moves to the ribosome of the cell, which then makes many copies of the RNA molecule. The information in each of these molecules is then used to manufacture the proteins that compose a virus particle. The copies of the RNA and proteins then reassemble into thousands more virus particles that then leave the host cell and move onto more cells.

It is amazing we know so much. Furthermore, we know the exact details of this genetic information. The RNA molecule in the SARS-CoV2 virus particle consists of a unique sequence of 33,000 letters (G, A, T, or C). In the laboratory, scientists can make a molecule with exactly this sequence and use these molecules to make artificial copies of the virus particles. We know so much. It is amazing. Aren't we clever! But there is more to the story!

The flu epidemic of 1918 to 1920 killed more people than World War I. Back then we did not even know that RNA existed, the structure of any protein molecule, what the genetic code was, the mechanism of infection, how to mathematically model the spread of epidemics, or the relative merits of different strategies for managing epidemics. We now know so much more. Today, this knowledge is saving thousands of lives.

Yet, we know so little. Although we know all the amazing details above, we cannot predict the structure of the virus particles. Furthermore, for some time we didn't know the design of effective and safe drugs and vaccines to treat COVID-19. We also don't really know how to balance the medical benefits and economic and social costs of lockdowns.

Modeling, understanding, and describing social, political, and economic phenomena, is even more difficult than physical, chemical, and biological phenomena. Scott E. Page is a professor of political science, complex systems, and economics at the University of Michigan. He teaches an online course, "Model Thinking," that has been taken by more than a million people. He makes the case for using multiple models to describe human behavior.[3] This reminds us that single solutions are not readily available.

We conclude, then, with a plea for humility and empathy. In constructing models of human behavior, a modeler must be humble. Given the challenges of diversity, social influence, cognitive errors, purpose, and adaptation, our models will inevitably be wrong or incomplete, which is why we take a many-model approach.

In 1932, Albert Einstein responded to a letter from Queen Elizabeth of Belgium, who complimented him on his lucid explanation to her of various topics in theoretical physics. He wrote: "It gave me great pleasure to tell you about the mysteries with which physics confronts us. As a human being, one has been endowed with just enough intelligence to be able to see clearly how utterly inadequate that intelligence is when confronted with what exists. If such humility could be conveyed to everybody, the world of human activities would be more appealing."[4]

The Science of Humility

Research over the past few decades, particularly studies in business and management, has shown that humility works. It is a powerful force for good and increases the chance of success in a range of human endeavors. Surprisingly to some, the meek do inherit the earth! John Dickson summarizes some of this social science research in his book *Humilitas: A Lost Key to Life, Love, and Leadership*. Dickson defines humility as follows:

3. Page, *The Model Thinker*, 58.
4. Quoted in Dukas and Hoffman, *Albert Einstein, The Human Side*, 48.

"Humility is *the noble choice to forgo your status, deploy your resources or use your influence for the good of others before yourself.* More simply, you could say the humble person is marked by *a willingness to hold power in service of others.* Humility presupposes your *dignity* . . . Humility is *willing.* It is a choice. Otherwise, it is humiliation . . . Humility is *social.* It is not a private act of self-deprecation . . . Humility is more about how I treat others than how I think about myself."[5]

Jim Collins was a professor at Stanford University when he led a large team who studied the characteristics of eleven highly successful companies. They discovered that each of these companies were led by distinct individuals, who he characterized as each a Level Five Executive who "builds enduring greatness through a paradoxical blend of personal humility and professional will."[6] In a *Harvard Business Review* article, Roger Martin, a professor of management at the University of Toronto, argues that the decline of a successful business is characterized by "the deterioration of necessary feedback" and then by a "proliferation of organization defensive routines." Managers "become impervious to learning of any kind." The antidote is listening and learning because "people are naturally scientific: they make hypotheses, collect information, criticize each other's demonstrated conclusions. The challenge is to channel this energy into an open discourse on the fate of the company, not into an underground discourse on the prejudices of the CEO."[7]

The value of making decisions based on a range of opinions is described by a concept in statistics and the social sciences known as "the wisdom of the crowd." It was first proposed in 1906 by the statistician Francis Galton after he observed a contest at a county fair to guess the weight of a slaughtered ox. The median guess from 800 participants was accurate within 1 percent of the true weight. Web resources such as Wikipedia, Quora, and Stack Exchange rely on collective human knowledge. The errors associated with individual human judgements are averaged out, provided the participants are truly diverse. There are well defined mathematical theorems to quantify and justify this perspective. Scott E. Page uses these to partially justify the many-models approach that he advocates in the social sciences. Furthermore, he has used a range of mathematical models and empirical

5. Dickson, *Humilitas*, 24–25. (Emphasis in the original.)

6. Collins, *Good to Great*, 185.

7. Martin, "Changing the Mind of the Corporation."

studies to argue the merits of decision-making in teams being based on the consideration of diverse opinions.[8]

In summary, it appears that research in the social sciences has shown that humility is a key to success in life. The meek do inherit the earth!

Biblical Perspectives on Humility

A pandemic can be a mirror of ourselves. Another mirror is the word of God (Jas 1:22–24). Turning from arrogance to humility is a theme that runs through the whole Bible. In the Old Testament, Israel was called upon to humble themselves before Yahweh and listen to his word. For example, the Lord said, "if my people who are called by my name humble themselves, and pray and seek my face and turn from their wicked ways, then I will hear from heaven and will forgive their sin and heal their land" (2 Chr 7:14 NIV—all Bible references in this chapter are NIV). Yet often Israel failed to humble themselves. Instead, they "did what was right in their own eyes." Consequently, they experienced conflict, affliction, and God's judgment.

John Dickson notes that the demands of humility expand significantly with the teaching of Jesus. In the Old Testament, Israel is called upon to be humble before God and before their leaders. However, in the New Testament, followers of Jesus must also be humble before others, including those of lower social status. Jesus concludes the parable of the Pharisee and the Tax Collector with the statement: "I tell you, this man went down to his house justified, rather than the other. For everyone who exalts himself will be humbled, but the one who humbles himself will be exalted" (Luke 18:14).

Central to a biblical perspective on humility is Philippians 2, where Jesus is cast as the model of humility: "And being found in human form, he humbled himself by becoming obedient to the point of death, even death on a cross" (Phil 2:8).

Dickson notes that the teachings of Jesus and Paul on humility represented a radical shift from those of the ancient world. This shift is the origin of why humility is so popular in the modern world. Dickson also argues that humility does not mean having a relativist position, that all views are equally valid. Rather, it means respecting and valuing people who have different views from our own.

8. Page, *The Diversity Bonus.*

A crisis should move us to be humble before God, before each other, and before nature (creation). This represents a partial reversal of the reordering of the world due to the fall. The first two chapters of Genesis describe God's intended world: one where there are harmonious ordered relationships between God, humans, and nature. However, the desire of Adam and Eve "to be like God" leads to disastrous consequences and a chaotic world where pain and violence multiply. There is a power struggle between man and woman, between humans and nature, and between humans and God.

Humility Before God

Humility leads to a greater sense of our creatureliness and our real identity. We are created by the Creator God. We are made in the image of God, but we are not God. We acknowledge our limitations: our finitude, our vulnerability, our dependence, and our sinful nature. This leads to repentance. Before God, we acknowledge our pride and rebellion. We cry out, "Lord, have mercy on me, a sinner." We also worship God for he is so much greater than us: sovereign, holy, righteous, loving, compassionate, just, and merciful.

"To whom shall we go?" To the one with the words of eternal life!

Humility Before Each Other

We acknowledge that every human is made in the image of God, regardless of gender, race, ethnicity, social status, wealth, power, religion, education, beliefs, family lineage, or achievements. We respect and value every one of those images. Humility means listening to others and valuing their perspective, including those we may disagree with. It includes being willing to listen to those with greater expertise and experience, whether virologists, climate scientists, pastors, or other community leaders. The letters of the Apostle Paul spell out the nature, practice, and basis of humility toward others. For example, he urges the Philippians, "Do nothing out of selfish ambition or vain conceit. Rather, in humility value others above yourselves, not looking to your own interests, but each of you to the interests of the others" (Phil 2:3–4).

Paul goes on to explain that the basis of this humility is the example of Christ's humility. Paul urges the members of the church in Rome: "Do not think of yourself more highly than you ought, but rather think of yourself with sober judgment" (Rom 12:3). This is because they are all members of the body of Christ. They need one another. They all have different gifts. Christ needs them all for the body to be complete and to show his "manifold wisdom" to the world. Humility before one another means acknowledging our interdependence.

Humility Before Nature

We mess with nature at our peril. Thomas Friedman is a columnist for *The New York Times* and has been an enthusiastic supporter of globalization. Yet, in a recent column he wrote:

> Covid-19 . . . is the logical outcome of our increasingly destructive wars against nature. As Johan Rockstrom, chief scientist at Conservation International, explains: "When you simultaneously hunt for wildlife and push development into natural ecosystems—destroying natural habitats—the natural balance of species collapses due to loss of top predators and other iconic species, leading to an abundance of more generalized species adapted to live in human dominated habitats. These are rats, bats and some primates—which together host 75 percent of all known zoonotic viruses to date, and who can survive and multiply in destroyed human dominated habitats."[9]

Since humans have become more numerous and concentrated in cities, and as deforestation has brought these generalized species closer to us—and as countries like China, Vietnam, and others in central Africa tolerated wet markets where these virus-laden species were mixed with domesticated meats—we are seeing ever more zoonotic diseases spreading from animals to people. Their names are SARS, MERS, Ebola, bird flu, and swine flu—and COVID-19. Add globalization to this and you have the perfect ingredients for more pandemics. We need to find a much more harmonious balance between economic growth and our ecosystems.

Nature is powerful and awesome. We cannot control cyclones, floods, droughts, or tsunamis. An unarmed human is no match for a grizzly bear, lion, or cobra. Furthermore, our understanding is limited. In the beautiful poetry of Job 38–40, God challenges Job to consider his place in nature and how that should lead Job to humble himself before God.

Humility before God, before one another, and before nature reflects the harmony of shalom. As Cornelius Plantinga writes:

9. Friedman, "We Need Herd Immunity from Trump and the Coronavirus."

> The webbing together of God, humans, and all creation in justice, fulfillment, and delight is what the Hebrew prophets call *shalom*. We call it peace, but it means far more than mere peace of mind or a cease-fire between enemies. In the Bible, shalom means *universal flourishing, wholeness, and delight*—a rich state of affairs in which natural needs are satisfied and natural gifts fruitfully employed, a state of affairs that inspires joyful wonder as its Creator and Savior opens doors and welcomes the creatures in whom he delights. Shalom, in other words, is the way things ought to be.[10]

Humility is a spiritual resource that helps us respond to a crisis. A crisis humbles us. We realize we are not as in control or as clever as we thought. We look to the sovereign and powerful God for help. We become open to the wisdom and expertise of others to help us find a way together through the crisis.

Blessed are the meek. They shall inherit the earth.

10. Plantinga, *Not the Way It's Supposed to Be*, 10.

Blessed are those who
hunger and thirst for righteousness,
for they will be filled.

Lord, you place within us a renewed passion,
a hunger and thirst for God's reign of righteousness and justice here on earth,
right in the midst of our upheavals.
You invite us into the self-emptying and sacrificial self-giving of the Trinity,
and through embracing your way of vulnerability,
we open ourselves to be filled by you.

4

Jesus' Invitation to Vulnerability

Irene Alexander

A pandemic holds up a mirror and helps us see what we really value, and what we hunger and thirst for. For those in the Christian tradition it might highlight where we are living at odds with our Christian faith. This helps us question whether we are living in response to the call of Jesus as the primary call on our lives, or whether we have been influenced by the culture of consumerism and individualism. What would it be like to live according to the Beatitudes, to live a life out of the love, faithfulness, and of vulnerability that Jesus, through his indwelling Spirit, has placed upon our hearts?

This chapter echoes the Beatitudinal call to hungering and thirsting for righteousness. The invitation is to learn to live Jesus' vulnerability in interdependent community, and to follow the cruciform and resurrectional movements of death with Christ to an old existence, and resurrection in him to new life. If, as Bonhoeffer says, the image of God is the image of Jesus Christ on the cross,[1] then we are also called to live a life of surrender and vulnerability, of knowing our security in God rather than money, of knowing ourselves loved for who we are rather than for a reputation, and of finding significance in community rather than in success. Thus, a third-century voice could still echo strongly amid our twenty-first-century pandemic crisis.

1. Cited in Baker, *The Cross of Reality*, 318.

Cyprian of Carthage, facing a terrifying plague in the 250s, wrote that the plague exposed how people viewed their lives in relation to God. It "reveals what we really care about, what we really love. The plague, in other words, makes visible what normally remains hidden in our ordinary lives of comfort and distraction."[2] What might Cyprian note about the West in this time of pandemic? He would surely notice, along with missiologist Lesslie Newbigin, that the church of the West is the most culturally captive of history. We are indeed living lives of comfort and distraction. By unmasking the lesser things for which we crave, the pandemic may call us back to living a life more focused on the kingdom of God, the vulnerable way of Jesus. Does this crisis time help us to open our hearts in receptivity to being formed and shaped by the Spirit of God, who waits at the edges of our lives and society to bring the wind of change and transformation?

Blessed are Those

Jesus' Sermon on the Mount is proclaiming an upside-down kingdom—or rather a call to live in the right-way-up kingdom, the way of Jesus. The Beatitudes—the characteristics of kingdom living that can flourish in our lives through the indwelling of Christ's Spirit—point us to what will bring satisfaction, enrichment, delight, and contentment,[3] unveiling a way of living that inverts much of our enculturation. It must have seemed countercultural to many of Jesus' first-century hearers, but how much more to those of us who live in the West? The first Beatitude addresses being poor in spirit—coming to God in a place of humility and painful awareness of our own neediness. This is not a usual stance for those of us growing up in the wealthy Western countries. We are used to relying on our own abilities, our money, and our power. Jesus calls us to the upside-down kingdom of emptying our hands and following him. If we are to truly take that journey, we will need to let go, to surrender our power, our reputation, and our desire to be in control. And as a result, we will be invited to mourn our losses, to become meek and to hunger and thirst for righteousness, that is, justice and goodness. This way of life is seeing things as God sees them.

2. Fogelman, "Fear as a Lack of Faith?"

3. See The Passion Translation of Matthew. The translator explains that in Aramaic—the language Jesus spoke—the word we have translated as "blessed" is so much richer than that one word.

Jesus is calling us to a higher way—a lower way—a way of poverty of spirit, of mourning our losses, of hungering and thirsting. And then, he says, we will obtain the kingdom of God, we will be comforted, we will be satisfied. David, the sweet psalmist of Israel (2 Sam 23:1), knew this God. One of his psalms, composed when he was hiding from Saul in a cave, claims, "I cry to God Most High, to God who fulfills his purpose for me" (Ps 57:2 NRSV). If we become dependent on God, surrender our self-reliance, trusting, in the face of crisis, the God most high, we will be satisfied, we will find what we most deeply long for. And we will experience the fulfillment of what we are designed for.

A scribe moved by Jesus' teaching cried out, "Teacher I will follow you wherever you go." But Jesus brings him back to reality, "Foxes have holes, and birds of the air have nests; but the Son of Man has nowhere to lay his head" (Matt 8:20 NRSV). Growing up in the West I have often heard a caveat with this kind of teaching: "It doesn't really mean . . ." But Paul and the disciples, and Francis of Assisi, and men and women through the ages have taken Jesus at his word, and laid down their lives and their possessions to follow Jesus. The invitation—and modeling—of Jesus is to surrender, to live in response to the Spirit, to give up homes, jobs, security, reputation, and control. Indeed, all our past cravings and poor attachments—to follow him, finding what our hearts most deeply desire.

We in the West have been like the Laodicean church claiming, "'I am rich, I have prospered, and I need nothing.' You do not realize that you are wretched, pitiable, poor, blind, and naked" (Rev 3:17 NRSV). When Peter reminds Jesus of what he has left to follow Jesus, Jesus responds, "And everyone who has left houses or brothers or sisters or father or mother or children or fields, for my name's sake, will receive a hundredfold" (Matt 19:20 NRSV). I read these words as a child, and took them literally—a call to follow Jesus rather than find security. And indeed, I have received a hundredfold—in friendships, in shared community, in shared life in countries other than my own, and among people around the world.

The Vulnerable Way of Jesus' Love and Faithfulness

The cruciform way of Jesus is a call to vulnerable living. It is a call to interdependence, to risk, and to admission of weakness. Jesus lived in dependence on others, which sometimes meant having nowhere to lay his head. He called his disciples, all of us, to follow him. Paul took the call seriously, traveling his known world, to take the good news of the kingdom. The good news that we can live depending on the Spirit.

When I was young, I joined Youth With A Mission—a missionary organization that encouraged its members to give up everything in following Jesus, and to join mission endeavors around the world. It was an exhilarating way to live—being in community, trusting God to show us the way forward, living without a steady income. It taught us much and freed us from the bondage of seeking security. I am presently part of an organization that lives even more vulnerably, seeking to follow the way of incarnation. I am an elder with them, rather than living the way they do. These men and women and families live in the slums alongside the poor as part of Servants to Asia's Urban Poor, trusting the pattern of the incarnation. They live alongside others is slum communities, to learn from them, and together to find ways to act justly and seek goodness. In his book *Slums Reimagined: How Informal Settlements Help the Poor Overcome Poverty,* Aaron Smith tells of how his family has chosen to live in a slum in Manila—and the richness of their life in that community.

The way of Jesus is the cruciform pattern of Philippians 2, Jesus, the Word from eternity past, "who, though he was in the form of God, did not regard equality with God as something to be exploited, but emptied himself, taking the form of a slave, being born in human likeness. And being found in human form, he humbled himself and became obedient to the point of death—even death on a cross" (Phil 2:6–8 NRSV). These words lay out the essence of the way of Jesus, the way of the "descending God."[4] Gordon Cosby, the founder of the Church of the Savior in Washington, explains that "it becomes plain to us that God has willed to show his love for the world by descending more and more deeply into human frailty . . . The truest symbols that we have of Jesus are the lamb—the lamb led to the slaughter, a sheep before its shearers being dumb. Total poverty: a dumb sheep, the Lamb of God, and the Servant Christ kneeling with a towel and a basin, washing feet on the eve of his crucifixion. The weeping Christ riding into Jerusalem on a donkey."[5] This is the image of the invisible God.

4. Cosby, *By Grace Transformed*, 29.

5. Cosby, *By Grace Transformed*, 29.

The Vulnerable God

Many times in the history of the West, Christians have preferred to focus on an ascending God, a God of power and might, and to make ourselves in that image. Paul tells us Jesus "is the divine portrait, the true likeness of the invisible God" (Col 1:15 TPT), and as Bonhoeffer expresses it, "The image of God is the image of Jesus Christ on the cross."[6] Any exploration as to what God is truly like brings us to the realization that our God is a vulnerable God. Maggie Ross, a present-day anchorite, spells it out thus: "The heart of Christianity is the self-emptying, kenotic humility of God expressed in Jesus the Christ . . . At the heart of God's humility is this: God willingly is wounded,"[7] "a kenotic living God who is unceasingly self-outpouring, compassionate, and engaged with the creation. . . . God's inviolable vulnerability, God's unswerving commitment to suffer with and within the creation, to go to the heart of pain, to generate new life, hope, and joy out of the cry of dereliction, out of the pain to utter self-denudation, utter self-emptying, utter engaging love."[8] Understanding the vulnerable God is recognizing that God chooses this way, not because God is powerless but because a kenotic God is *more* powerful. As Maggie Ross concludes: "The question is not God's power (whether God is omnipotent) but God's *use* of power."[9] God's choice of shared power, power *with* rather than power *over*, invites us also to responsibility and openness, to hunger and thirst for goodness and justice in this world. We are called to an incarnational participation to the life and purposes of this vulnerable God.

Living in Vulnerability

Paul articulates this vulnerable way of living for us. "Our strength is made perfect in weakness 'My grace is always more than enough for you, and my power finds its full expression through your weakness.' So I will celebrate my weaknesses, for when I'm weak I sense more deeply the mighty power of Christ living in me" (2 Cor 12:9 TPT). Earlier in the same letter he had pictured the image of us as common clay jars, with the "brilliant dawning light of the glorious knowledge of God" (2 Cor 4:6 TPT) being seen to be

6. Bonhoeffer, *The Cost of Discipleship*, 231.
7. Ross, *Pillars of Flame*, xvi.
8. Ross, *Pillars of Flame*, 72.
9. Ross, *Pillars of Flame*, 203–4.

of God and not of us. This is the call to the vulnerable way—to be seen for who we are, flawed and human, but walking in union with a God who is all love. Theologian Michael Gorman spells out this call to us from the vulnerable God to the body of Christ, the followers of Jesus: "the self-emptying (kenotic), self-humbling, self-giving, vulnerable, and 'downwardly mobile' God revealed in Christ crucified generates a self-emptying (kenotic), self-humbling, self-giving, vulnerable, 'downwardly mobile' community of people in Christ."[10] This is not the first way I learned the gospel.

I grew up reading the Bible and I wanted to be a good little girl. It was startling as an adult to read from Gary Hayachi that the gospel is not a "paradigm of evaluation, it is not about being good, it's about being real."[11] I realized that I had bought into the idea that being a Christian was about living by a moral code, obeying the legal principles of the Old (and New) Testament, that in some ways I was more like the Pharisees than the followers of Jesus, more like the older brother in the story of the prodigal son, out in the fields working, and evaluating myself as better than others. I rediscovered the creation story to be an invitation to live in relationship with God, the tree of life; a lived and responsive relationship with the Spirit, rather than eating of the tree of knowledge of good and evil—trying to "be like God, knowing good and evil" (Gen 3:5 NRSV) within my own being.

The paradigm of evaluation is the false self, constantly evaluating how to be good, how to know good and evil, how to be better than others, how to measure up. The false self is a defended self, a person behind a mask, trying to live up to the requirements, only showing to others what they might consider acceptable. The true gospel is an invitation to let the masks drop, to fall into the arms of the God of unconditional love, to let ourselves be seen for who we are. Richard Rohr points out that it is the broken ones in the Gospel stories who hang around Jesus—the tax collectors and the prostitutes, not the Pharisees.[12] And it is the broken part of myself that will help me find Jesus. That part of myself that knows I don't have it all together, that I need the Spirit to hold me in relationship with God, masks dropped, true, vulnerable self known. While this might sound very scary, especially to religious people, it is the way to freedom. It is the way of poverty of spirit, of hungering and thirsting, and finding what we most truly long for. Jesus told his followers, "Unless your righteousness exceeds that of the scribes and

10. Gorman, *Participating in Christ*, 63.

11. Hayachi, Living Waters seminar.

12. Rohr, *True Self, False Self.*

Pharisees, you will never enter the kingdom of Heaven" (Matt 5:20 NRSV). This has often been heard as Jesus creating an even higher moral code than that of the Pharisees. But in the spirit of the Sermon on the Mount it is calling us to a *different* way, a different kind of righteousness—in an inner life of integrity[13] and vulnerability.

The inner life is often represented in the cartoons of Australian artist, Michael Leunig. He acknowledges: "I'm being taught how to be frail and why perhaps in the end that's one of the most profound and rewarding things one can do."[14] Leunig is known for his conversations of his cartoon man and the Duck—a representation of the soul. In a cartoon drawn during the pandemic the man makes the following rather panicky statements, and the Duck responds from a place of calm realism but with profound knowing:

> The world is changing. The Duck: It's always changing
>
> Our lives are in danger. We are in lockdown. The Duck: Life is always dangerous. We were never free.
>
> Many of us could die. The Duck: We all get our turn.
>
> Nobody knows what's going to happen. The Duck: Nobody *ever* knows. This makes life interesting.
>
> We don't know what to believe anymore. The Duck: Keep an open mind. This also makes life interesting.
>
> We are living in strange times. The Duck: When were we *not* living in strange times.[15]

The Duck holds up the mirror of reality, whereas the man shows how most of us live in illusion, which the pandemic has stripped away from us. We are invited to live vulnerably in a vulnerable world. There is something very appealing in Leunig's vulnerable characters. They find life too hard, but they step out of the rat race to find the reality of a vulnerable world where those who wait in silence begin to find healing for their souls.

As a spiritual director I have the privilege of hearing this attractiveness also. In the sacred space of spiritual companioning people tell their stories, sometimes stories they have never told before, allowing themselves

13. The Passion translates Matthew 5:20 "unless your lives are more pure and full of integrity . . ."

14. Leunig, "The Leunig Fragments."

15. Leunig, "The World is Changing."

to be unmasked and seen for who they really are—their inner beauty is revealed. This is contrary to the societal myth that says we will be rejected and shamed if we reveal our real selves.

The interaction of shame and vulnerability has been researched by Brené Brown. Her TED talk *The Power of Vulnerability* is one of the five most viewed TED talks in the world. Our upbringing and culture have told us that vulnerability brings feelings of shame, fear, and uncertainty. "Yet," says Brown, "we too often lose sight of the fact that vulnerability is also the birthplace of joy, belonging, creativity, authenticity, and love."[16] She notes that people try hard to shield themselves from disappointment and shame by making an armor of cynicism and numbness, but that this self-defense comes at great cost. She explains how much richer our lives would be if we could open ourselves to vulnerability, to "showing up and letting ourselves be seen," that this is a true measure of our courage.

The way of vulnerability is not only the healthier way for an individual to live—it is essential for community, especially when living for the kingdom of God, reflecting as it does the mutual self-giving of the persons of the Trinity.

Vulnerability and Interdependence

Crises have a way of bringing out the best and the worst in people. One of the obvious positive outcomes of the pandemic has been the extent to which people have begun to know their neighbors, the way people have found ways to show their gratitude for the medical community, the creativity with which people have found ways to connect with others in need, the energy people have spent in seeking goodness and justice. The flip side has been the exposing of our selfishness, our fear, our desire to hoard as if we lived in a culture of greed and scarcity.

One of the gifts of living in Asian countries is the experience of living in a communal culture. A communal culture values the relationship, the community, over the individual. This can sound scary for those of us who have grown up in individualistic societies, where we have learned to claim our possessions, our space, our reputation. Communal cultures are much more open to sharing, to sharing their needs, as well as sharing what they have. Capitalist societies tend to see everything in terms of profitability as the bottom line, whereas communal societies see the value

16. Brown, *The Power of Vulnerability*.

of the family and their relationships. Mohamad Safa, a permanent representative at the United Nations, names our tendency to see the world in economic terms. "It took a pandemic," he says, "for the world to finally understand we live in a society, not an economy."[17] Here is an echo of the call of the kingdom of God. If the pandemic could indeed teach us that, it would be worth the hard lesson it has been.

Paul in his many New Testament letters writes to the church. Almost every time he uses the word "you" it is in the plural form—he is speaking to the church, that is, the gathered people, the community. He sees himself as a steward in the household of God (Col 1:25). The word household in Greek is *oikos*, from which the word *economy* is drawn.[18] *Oikos* in the New Testament was the recognition that we are all part of God's household, where we share what we have as a family, the household of faith. This same Greek word *oikos* is the root word of ecology—the recognition that we are stewards of the earth that God has created and given to us to care for (Gen 1:28).

Our Interdependence with Creation

Larry Rasmussen in *Earth-Honoring Faith* addresses the idea of the *oikos* as the "world-house," and calls us to a new economic ethos that would "reject freedom as unrestrained political and market individualism and cultivate freedom as thriving in community in ways that contribute to personal well-being and the common good, including the goods of the commons (soil, air, water, energy)." [19]

If a pandemic can teach us we are a community not an economy, could it also teach us that we are part of the community that includes creation? Could we seek justice and goodness not only for our society but also for our earth? We have been called to this for decades, indeed longer. Over fifty years ago, essayist Wendell Berry wrote, "We have lived our lives by the assumption that what was good for us would be good for the world . . . We have been wrong. We must change our lives so that it will be possible to live by the contrary assumption, that what is good for the world will be good for us. And that requires that we make the effort to *know* the world and learn what is good for it."[20] Indigenous peoples all over the world have watched

17. Safa, on Twitter.

18. Conradie, *Christianity and Earthkeeping*, 115.

19. Rasmussen, *Earth-Honoring Faith*, 148.

20. Berry, *The Long Legged House*, 220.

with horror as outsiders have ruined the environment. An Osage proverb says: "When the last tree is cut down, the last fish eaten, and the last stream poisoned, you will realize that you cannot eat money."

Climate change is making response to the environment an urgent demand. Can the pandemic cause a pause-button all over the world, a call to be silent and take stock, a call to reevaluate our lifestyle and choose what is good and just for the world? As we choose vulnerability, as we choose to hunger and thirst for God's kingdom on this earth, we learn to live in community, to find our true identity in being seen for who we are, and becoming a people who care for our neighbor, our world, and for the other.

A Liturgy for Vulnerability

Call to prayer:

Trust in God at all times, people

Pour out your hearts to the Holy One

For God alone my soul waits in silence

(Pause)

Theme:

Our vulnerability. God's identification with our weakness and vulnerability. God's presence and kindness.

Prayer

God, Creator of the stars and the sun, present before the worlds began, we acknowledge that you too are the creator of the little things.

We see in you the tenderness of the mother and the protectiveness of the father, the playfulness of children, and the humor of human beings everywhere.

We see you in Jesus, the image of the invisible God. We recognize you as the Crucified One, the one led like a lamb to death. And yet you also are the Risen One.

We know in our own lives how you speak to us in the inner whisper of our hearts, the brush of a breeze on our cheek, the warmth of the sun on our faces. We recognize the nudge of your Spirit in gentle and sensitive movements, your responsiveness to our musings, your Scriptures that nourish our hearts.

We come to you God of openness and vulnerability, to learn of you, and to follow in your ways.

Song

O Lord hear my prayer, O Lord hear my prayer,

When I call answer me . . . Come and listen to me.—Taizé[1]

Readings: All or some of the following:

Judges 6:1–16, Ruth 1:1–19, Philippians 2:5–8, 2 Corinthians 4:5–10

Invitation to reflection on Bible stories where God used the vulnerable.

Times in our own lives where God has responded to us in our vulnerability

Our images of God and the invitation to see God in the face of the Crucified One

Poem: Immanence

I come in the little things,

Saith the Lord;

My starry wings I do forsake,

Love's highway of humility to take;

Meekly I fit my stature to your need.

In beggar's part

About your gates I shall not cease to plead

As man, to speak with man

1. Taizé Reflections, "O Lord Hear my Prayer."

Till by such art
I shall achieve my immemorial plan;
Pass the low lintel of the human heart.[2]

Benediction:

God before me, God behind me
God above me, God below me;
I on the path of God,
God upon my track

Who is there on land?
Who is there on wave?
Who is there on billow?
Who is there by doorpost?
Who is along with us? God and Lord.

I am here abroad,
I am here in need,
I am here in pain,
I am here in straits,
I am here alone. O God aid me.[3]

2. Underhill, *The Augusten Books of Poetry*, 5.
3. Ringma and Alexander, eds., *Of Martyrs*, 124.

Blessed are the merciful,

for they will receive mercy.

Lord, we live under your wide and tender mercy

with all aspects of our lives mattering to you.

You enliven within us a spirit of mercy and compassion reflective of your own,

so that those around us matter as they matter to you.

Mercy and compassions are marks of our kingdom character.

You invite us to care deeply and soulfully for others,

to pray for them and be present to them,

knowing that we are eternally enfolded in your loving embrace.

5

Stay with me. Watch and pray.

Tim McCowan

Be merciful, just as your Heavenly Father is merciful (Luke 6:36 NIV).

God blesses those who are merciful, for they will be shown mercy (Matt 5:7 NLT).

We had just arrived at our rural cottage for our long-awaited holiday. Having explored the rooms and unpacked our bags, my wife and I then made our way to the supermarket for some supplies for the week. As we came into a roundabout, a large utility truck ploughed into the front passenger side of our little sedan. The utility driver was very apologetic, saying the bright sunshine in his eyes meant he didn't see our vehicle. Very fortunately no one was hurt, but our little blue Corolla was badly damaged. A minor crisis, but one that could affect not just our holiday, but the rest of our lives, depending on how we would respond.

A crisis can be a like a car crash. Something suddenly hits us from the side and derails our lives, perhaps takes away our job or income, a loved one, a dream, or our health. The coronavirus pandemic has certainly been like this. Hundreds of thousands have died, lost their jobs, livelihoods, and we don't know what life, or the world, will look like after it's over. What does it mean to be merciful to those who are suffering?

In the midst of the rapid spread and tragedy of so many dying from the virus, I heard other distressing news. The young son of friends, Jenny and Rob, had died in a terrible car crash.[1] Tony was only eighteen. Rob is so upset and angry at God that he doesn't want to talk with anyone about it. Jenny is distraught, carrying her own grief, and struggling with Rob's withdrawal and the stress on their relationship. Then I learned that Michael, a member of our church community, is in a coma after being hit by a car while cycling to work. His wife, Fiona, and daughter, Diane, now struggling with shock, face a very unknown future. Another friend, Kathy, lost her son Richard to cancer, after a seven-year battle. How can I express God's mercy toward these loved ones with the pandemic's strict social distancing restrictions in place?

Then news of the virus in the majority world started to pour in, including the Philippines, a country where I serve and have many friends and colleagues. Most of my friends are reliant on a daily wage to feed their familes, and live in informal settlements where social distancing is impossible. Within two months, nearly 1,000 Filipinos had died, and 10 percent of these deaths were healthcare professionals. Sadly, the situation is exacerbated by the heavy-handed governmental response. In imprisoning offenders of the lockdown restrictions, further outbreaks of the virus are likely in the overcrowded prisons. And no financial support has been offered for those who have lost livelihoods and cannot feed their families. What does being merciful to these vulnerable ones in a national crisis look like?

At a societal level we've been reminded of the ongoing injustices of racial discrimination and institutional abuse of human rights, particularly of the poor and marginalized. Those instruments of state, the police, the judiciary, laws, and many of the current systems of governance, have, instead of supporting human life and flourishing, been like a big utility truck, cruelly and unjustly smashing the lives of those of different color or ethnicity, religion or sexual orientation, and the vulnerable poor. The Black Lives Matter protests in the US resonated with millions of colored peoples around the world, including First Nations peoples, exposing injustices, abuses of power, and the widespread racial discrimination that underlies them. What is called for from followers of Jesus in these circumstances? Is a merciful response just about caring for the victims, or does it also involve stopping the violence of the "big utility trucks" of the State, and the racist mind-sets that drive them?

Climate scientists have been warning us that we are living in the midst of a planetary crisis, that could see the earth uninhabitable for

1. Names have been changed to protect their identities.

humans in a hundred years if we don't take action now.[2] Time is critical. Could this crisis be like an unfolding car crash, that still affords a little time to change our direction to avoid total disaster? To put our foot on the vehicle's brake, in order to respond more wisely, with greater awareness of the whole planet's vulnerable ecosystem? What is our Christian response to this crisis? Does being merciful involve listening to the wisdom of scientists and the best of our Christian tradition, to repent of our excessive consumption patterns, and live more justly, sustainably, and kindly, especially towards our future generations?

When faced with persons in need, I want to respond mercifully, to alleviate their distress. I feel uncomfortable seeing a loved one in acute pain, deep grief, or despair. So I respond, hoping to ease their suffering with the best of intentions. However, sometimes my responses have had poor outcomes. I may have assumed their need was one thing, when actually it was another. And sometimes my response has arisen more from a desire to be relieved of the uncomfortable emotions than the other person's need.

So facing these multiple crises, and learning of the diverse needs of friends and neighbors here and afar, I started asking God how I should respond. What does it mean to be merciful, as your Heavenly Father is merciful, in these circumstances? I felt drawn to reflect upon Jesus' experience of suffering in the garden of Gethsemane (Matt 26:36–46; Mark 14:32–43; Luke 22:39–46).[3]

Jesus was in agony. His sorrow was crushing the life out of him (Matt 26:38, The Message). In facing the inevitability of his betrayal by his friends, the trial and gruesome execution at the hands of a brutal empire, the vulnerability of his still fledgling movement, plus the end of all he had worked and prayed for, Jesus sought out two things. In his acute distress, he wanted time alone with his Father, and he desired the supportive presence of his friends.

In Matthew 29:38–41 we read: "'My soul is exceedingly sorrowful, even to death. Stay here and watch with me.' He went a little farther and fell on his face, and prayed, saying, 'O my Father, if it is possible, let this cup pass from me; nevertheless, not as I will, but as you will.' Then he came to the disciples and found them sleeping, and said to Peter, 'What!

2. United Nations, "The Climate Crisis."

3. Jesus' agony in the garden is recounted in all the Synoptic Gospels: Matt 26:36–46; Mark 14:32–42; Luke 22:39–46.

Could you not watch with me one hour? Watch and pray, lest you enter into temptation'" (NKJV).

For Jesus, turning to his Abba was his natural first response, whether in a crisis or not. He knew time with this Merciful One who was always with him, forever attentive, and offering genuine understanding and wisdom, would strengthen him. He could pour out the crushing weight of sorrow to this One, without fear of reprimand. Abba knew his needs and listened mercifully as a good Father, without being critical, impatient, or judgmental.[4] Jesus was completely open and honest about his struggle, and his desire that this hour would pass. He persevered in this wrestling with God, repeating his request, but affirming "yet I want your will to be done, not mine" (Matt 26: 39, 42, 44; Mark 14:36). There is no indication that Jesus received any verbal response, even after three hours. Yet, he emerged from this time clear and ready for what lay immediately ahead. He trusted Abba, wanting his will to be aligned with his Father's.

In my early years as a Christian, I learned to petition God for what I needed. So I made my requests known to God, committing them into his care. I thought trusting God meant that after I had named them, even briefly, I should let them go, move on. To linger with them was tantamount to doubting his care of me. Occasionally I would add an "If it be your will." But in hindsight, I see that many of my prayers were based on what I thought was needed, rather than truly waiting and listening to discern God's desire.

Jesus' openness to God in the garden reminds me that prayer is more about entrusting myself and all things to God rather than claiming what I want. His loving trust in Abba convinces me to be more open and honest with God, not just about what I desire but also what I fear. Jesus' surrender to his Father's desire challenges me to stay prayerfully waiting with God and listening for the Spirit until my desires are aligned with God's. Jesus' pleas to God also remind me that prayer can be more a vigorous wrestling with emotional distress than a cozy fireside chat.

Yet time alone with his Father was not enough in this crisis. Jesus was in such need that he requested the support of his close friends.[5]

4. See Crossan, *The Greatest Prayer*, especially 40–52.

5. Such an interpretation underscores Jesus' full humanity, revealing him as a vulnerable being in acute distress.

Stay With Me

I used to think that Jesus' request was just for the physical support of friends, to assure him that he was not facing such horrible events alone. Yet, as I have reflected upon my own experiences of distress and of supporting others in theirs, I now believe he was requesting something far more than this.

I resonate with Jesus' plea. When I am suffering a crisis like in a car crash, I want a friend near me. A person I trust who can ground me, steady me when I feel shaky, and be a sounding board for when decisions are to be made. Someone who will be attentive to what is going on in me and around me, and not be distracted or turn away when things get messy or even traumatic. I want their full, undivided presence, watching and praying with me.

To be a presence that is fully attentive and undivided is how I interpret Jesus' request to "stay here with me." Hence his great disappointment when the disciples fell asleep instead of staying awake and attentive. This level of presence to people is how I believe Jesus ministered to people.[6] Mark Yaconelli calls this the contemplative way. Jesus' way of "being with God within the reality of the present moment . . . It's about attentiveness—opening our eyes to God, ourselves, and others. Contemplation is an attitude of the heart, an all-embracing hospitality to what is."[7]

Besides being a means of spiritual support, Jesus' request was also a holy gift that he was sharing with these friends. He was trusting them with his deep distress and crushing sorrow, and opening a window into the dynamics of love in his most intimate relationship, and what it means to desire God's will more than one's own (Matt 6:9–10). If they could learn to persevere in watchful prayer and attentive presence to him through his intense and painful wrestling with God, then they would surely have been less inclined to flee or react with violence when the attackers eventually came (Matt 26:50–56). Jesus' response to the unfolding violence was grounded in a deeper trust that his Father's will was best, and would sustain him. This important lesson was part of his spiritual formation of his disciples. Molding them into a people who live the Love that he shared, and allowing his prayer to become their prayer, his life their life, his will their will.

This is not at all to discount the emotional, spiritual, and physical challenges of staying alert and present to him for three or more hours. I have learned the difficulties and challenges in trying to remain present to

6. Yaconelli, *Contemplative Youth Ministry*, 24.

7. Yaconelli, *Contemplative Youth Ministry*, 23.

people in acute distress. It requires divine grace to maintain such presence; I don't believe it's possible in one's own strength.

Watch

Jesus requested his friends not only to stay, but to "keep watch with me" (v. 38), and "keep alert" and pray (v. 41). His command is countercultural when my usual practice is to shut my eyes, in order to close off distractions and maintain my focus on God's Spirit within me. This is a stern warning not to withdraw from whatever painful realities are before me, and not to retreat into my own private world.

Jesus exhorts his followers to watch nine times in the Gospels. The word is sometimes translated as "stay awake" or "be alert." We are to watch for we do not know the hour the master of the house will return (Mark 13:34–37), and be alert for the robber whenever he comes (Matt 24:42–43), suggesting a constant awareness or mindfulness to what is occurring even during the night. The writer of Ephesians uses the same word to urge the church to stay alert, ready for assault from powers of evil (Eph 6:18). In the first epistle of Peter, believers are exhorted to be "watchful" for "your adversary the devil prowls around like a roaring lion, seeking someone to devour" (1 Pet 5:8). There is a sense that watching involves an inner alertness to resist those spirits, voices, or forces of evil that seek to steal one's attention or to do violence, injustice, or evil in the world.[8]

The importance of Jesus' exhortation becomes clearer when juxtaposed with the disciples' sleepiness. They fall asleep; unable to remain aware of all that is happening for Jesus. They were surely tired. However, his rebuke shows he sought more than just their open eyes. He and they faced sociocultural, political, and spiritual powers that needed to be "seen" by this inward watchfulness and then nonviolently engaged.

This watching and praying is not passive. To stay with a person in distress or to confront social injustices or institutions abusing children or the vulnerable, when so many "voices" (internal and external) cry out to leave, is an extremely active thing to do. Such contemplative action was possible for Jesus after his intense prayer, but was beyond the ability of his followers. Many of them fled, and Peter struck out with his sword (Matt 29:51). They did not have the inner resources to address the unfolding violent scenario,

8. Wink, *The Powers That Be.*

when it seemed that all their hopes about Jesus being a victorious Messiah were crumbling before their eyes.

Pray

Jesus exhorts his friends to pray. I do not doubt he knew Abba's Love, but sometimes when distress is great, one needs another to hold the light of God for you.[9] He wanted them close, attentive rather than asleep, and prayerful, perhaps as a way to keep him steady and grounded in his calling to the cross in Jerusalem. For them it was to keep holding the prayerful gaze of God's Love on him, as a way to keep him grounded in that Love himself.

Jesus' exhortation is linked with the phrase: "so you will not fall into temptation" (Matt 26:41; Mark 14:38), which ties into his teaching in the Lord's Prayer (Matt 6:13). This suggests that we face temptations to turn away from being attentive to the present reality, and to avoid what is occurring for those in a crisis, whether it be personal, social, or global.

I know something of these temptations. Reality is often too painful, the sorrow too heavy, the powers that be too intimidating, and I want to run away. I feel powerless and helpless to change the situation. I know I cannot save another person from their crisis. I cannot repair Jenny and Rob's broken relationship, or return Kathy's dead son, or bring Fiona's husband out of his coma, or stop the racial prejudice or prevent a government from making unwise decisions. These are beyond my human control.

I think it is significant that Jesus wanted his friends close by, but not to intervene. He did not ask them to rescue him or console him in his distress. He was not asking them to deliver him from the predicament of this "hour," nor to counsel him to take a different course of action. His request was simple: stay here with me, watch and pray. In other words, no "action" needed. Jesus' response when the disciples do try to defend him from the authorities underscores the importance of not trying to take matters into one's own hands. Such efforts and impulsive reactions often lead to violence. Jesus reprimands them strongly. He reminds them of what he reaffirmed in the garden: that he would trust in God's power and the greater good of his will in each situation (Matt 26:53–54). They were to stay with him but at a distance, to watch attentively to what he and they were experiencing, and to pray, remaining connected with Abba themselves. So

9. An adaptation of the words from "The Servant Song", © Richard Gillard. Universal Music, 1997.

this "non-interventionist" request of Jesus is teaching me a new way to be merciful to those who suffer.

Participating in God's Mercy

Gerald May, a Christian psychiatrist, illuminates this manner of demonstrating mercy through the analogies of healing and growth.[10] He says healing and growth are natural processes that occur within the human body, given the right conditions and support. All the resources needed for these processes to unfold are found within the person or the environment; the only requirement of outsiders, whether doctors treating wounds or parents bringing up children or gardeners caring for plants, is to foster the conditions of "naturalness," "cleanliness," and "rest," so that the normal healing or growth can occur more fully.[11]

As I read the Gospels, I perceive Jesus ministering to people with similar assumptions. Namely, that the Spirit of God was already working within the people, it didn't need to be brought in from outside. For example, Jesus often says your faith has saved you (Matt 9:22; 29; Mark 5:34; 10:52; Luke 7:50; 18:42). Or, "let it be to you according to your faith" (Matt 9:29). He sees the faith of those carrying the man who was paralyzed and says he is forgiven (Mark 2:5). He seemed to be releasing the healing power of the Spirit already present in the situation, rather than introducing something external and new into their bodies. However, he also confronted attitudes of judgment, doubt, fear, self-righteousness, and jealousy that could hinder the Spirit's healing (Matt 7:1–5; 12:22–32; Mark 3:1–6; Luke 7:36–50; 13:10–17; John 5:1–18; 9:1–41). These attitudes act like toxins that can infect a wound; they impede the healing energies of life and love, the naturalness, cleanliness, and rest that bring about healing.

With this outlook, I understand Jesus' request to his friends as helping him to stay connected with his Father (naturalness), not interfering with his struggle through introducing their own fears and agendas (cleanliness), and giving him the safe space to express himself as honestly and fully as he needed (rest). All Jesus required in moving through his crisis was available within him and in his relationship with Abba. The disciples' presence was invited to support him in staying centered in that relationship.

10. May, *Simply Sane*, ch. 8, "True Growth and Healing."

11. May, *Simply Sane*, 74–76.

This teaches me that my attitude to another in crisis is to be one of participating with God, rather than making things happen, and trying not to interfere in the God-given processes of healing and growth that are already present. So I understand my prayers now as seeking to create the right conditions for God's Spirit to work in me and others; whether this is to heal, deliver, or liberate those who are oppressed.

This approach informs how I attempt to show mercy to those who are suffering. Previously, I assumed I needed to alleviate my neighbor's distress, like the good Samaritan (Luke 10:30–37). This puts the spotlight on me, the "giver," and can cause the recipient to feel patronized, treated as an object of pity and disempowered. However, this new understanding of being merciful can involve me watching (being attentive) to how God's Spirit is already at work in their situation to bring healing or reconciliation, before participating in that work. This ensures the other person's dignity and the wider community's wisdom is respected.

So, what am I called to do? How might Jesus' request guide me in how to mercifully support and intercede for others and myself in these situations of crisis? As I pray for my friends, my intention is to stay attentive to God's Spirit within me. I desire to reflect back God's love through prayer, spoken and unspoken, hoping for them to connect with God's presence within them. I watch to prevent any thought, spirit, or internal voice from diverting me from remaining present to their harsh reality, and any temptation to rely on my own strength, fix their problems, or advise them prematurely of what they should do. My prayer is also for the grace to not impede God's mercy flowing out to them, since this is what provides the strength and hope to persevere through crises. And I seek to trust God's desire and mercy for the greater good of all, as Jesus did.

My prayer, if it is genuine, will flow into my life, and vice versa. Thus, I seek to be as attentive to these friends and their needs, physically when I am with them, or when I am interceding alone. So when visiting Jenny and Rob, I listen as actively and as mercifully as I can to their agony, distress, pain, and struggle. I seek to reflect God's love back to them, prayerfully hoping they will return to that place of God within.

My wife and I drop around to Fiona, to let her know we are present to her during this uncertain future, while Michael is in the coma. We listen attentively as she shares of the painful, stressful, and sleepless weeks she has experienced. We gaze with God's unconditional love at her, seeking to foster the Spirit's mercy within her, that will help her go on. We remain watchful for any temptation to divert her or us from residing in that center of God's Love. Do our prayers wake Michael up from his coma? I would like to believe our prayers evoke the flow of life and love that is in him.

And when we attend to Kathy, grieving for her son Richard who died of cancer, we open up our hearts to all she is experiencing. We seek not to impede the flow of mercy back to her, and prayerfully trust she will be able to stay centered in that place of God's Love within.

How do I pray for those experiencing the nationwide crisis in the Philippines? I ask for the grace to be "with them" spiritually if not physically, and to be guided in what I pray. I want my intercession to foster the conditions for healing the fabric of their society and to support those most vulnerable. I pray they would be attentive to both the virus and the sources of God's life within their culture, and watchfully resist reactions that can infect the healing taking place. And I partner with others to share financial support towards those who have lost their livelihoods, as an expression of being merciful.

Does this approach change how I respond to those families of color who have suffered racially inspired violence and injustice at the hands of the state? Yes. I realize I first need to come alongside and listen attentively to their pain, justified anger, and distress, before taking any action "on their behalf." I hear Jesus inviting me to watch for and resist the evil one's influence, including repenting of attitudes of white male superiority that have unjustly privileged me over those from different backgrounds, and caused such violence. And I seek to partner with their communities to bring those attitudes into wider consciousness, and nonviolently engage the systems of the State to foster justice for all.

And our planet in its climate crisis? What if God was inviting us to come alongside our planet in its crisis, in order to listen deeply to its God-given wisdom until our hearts become more aligned with Abba's heart for her? This might foster our growth as his agents for healing and reconciliation rather than agents of destruction.

Ultimately, I believe all genuine prayer like this leads us into the deeper desire of God for each of us. Denis Edwards summarizes:

> While the Christian tradition affirms the central importance of asking God for the specific and everyday things we need; it also affirms that ultimately there is "one thing" we need to ask for: the grace of being drawn more deeply into the love of God. Of course, to ask for this gift is risky. We risk being drawn into boundless

> love. There is much in us that resists such love. But we can come to know our own resistance, and we can pray for freedom, knowing that the Spirit of God not only prays in us but also frees us to receive the gift offered to us.[12]

This chapter has reflected on Jesus' prayer and request of his friends in Gethsemane, out of the conviction that it reveals something of God's desire for us, both personally and communally, at all times. When we open to this desire, we discover the grace to be merciful toward others, and enfold them in our prayer to our Heavenly Father.

12. Edwards, *How God Acts*, 177–78.

Blessed are the pure in heart,
for they will see God.

Lord, you redeem our hearts, reconcile them to you,
and transform them into the likeness of your own transparent heart.
It is through the gift of your indwelling presence
that we are invited to look at ourselves and others,
through your eyes and through the Spirit-illuminated eyes of our hearts.
Lord, help us to discern your presence
amid the crises and upheavals of our day so that we can see you more clearly,
love you more dearly, and follow you more nearly.

6

In-Christ, In Crisis: The Painful Maturity of Love

Paul Mercer

It was a cold, dark evening. A drizzle had set in as I left the building, and hurried to my car. It had been another full day; indeed, most days have had a crammed feeling since the COVID-19 pandemic entered our daily reality and consciousness. This nanoparticle enemy has reset everyone's adreno-cortical axis toward the red zone.

This afternoon, a call came from an aged care facility, concerned that a resident had developed a painful rash. Shingles simply loves rising cortisol levels. In lockdown, with the COVID-19 contagion lurking, herpes zoster took its chance and jagged across the buttock. A recent room change for my patient could also have contributed. God only knows, but I prescribed a viral antibiotic to put out its fire, and started for home. Hunger rumblings were traveling with me, but I punted for delayed gratification and turned on the radio. In truth, it was a twenty-four-hour COVID-19 news fix that I needed. Zoster fire was rapidly replaced by a terrible news fact! Notifications for child abuse in Australia had nearly trebled since pandemic restrictions had been introduced and dark web servers were crashing from high traffic flows. O, Lord, deliver us from evil!

My wife is very family oriented. We share our home with our youngest daughter's family. The pandemic has demanded adjustments around travel and hygiene to keep us all safe. For me, work was now a mix of telehealth and face-to-face encounters where everyone is screened. Nearly everyone has risen to these new demands of civility, yet my time out of the home represents risk. I got out of the car, left my shoes at the door, and received the welcome of home. I was a little surprised by the enquiry, "Would you like your dinner now?" The normal expectation was to shower and allow the detergent quality of soap to knock down any lingering COVID-19 clusters. The grip of my day, fueled by the sadness of rising child abuse, must have left an impression on my face. I thankfully ate, showered, and sat down. We chatted together. There have been worse days.

How can we maintain a pure heart with all the pressures and change imposed by our defensive struggle against this SARS2 pathogen? Indeed, in any crisis in life?

My evenings during the pandemic have been made lighter by joining in prayer with medical colleagues. WhatsApp was not around during the Spanish flu epidemic in 1917. This elegant software makes the modern mobile phone sing praises to God. From around Australia and, at times, internationally, we have logged on and prayed together. We have lamented. We have shared our fears. We have rejoiced to share stories of grace. The therapeutic index of this corporate prayer has felt very strong. Tonight, the viral harmony had counted me out of WhatsApp prayer, so I turned to read.

Rowan Williams was musing about "the painful maturity of love."[1] The following words struck me as true. "Knowledge of God is not a subject's conceptual grasp of an object; it is sharing what God is—more boldly you might say, sharing God's experience. God is known in and by the exercise of crucifying compassion. If we are like him in that, we know him. And we know 'as we are known.'"[2] Here was a choice wine of the Holy Spirit serving a nightcap for my day. Here was a mirror where I could see the footprints of Jesus sharing the presence of consultations, the compassion of Jesus sighing with me in the middle of the moans of life.

When I started to reflect on the meaning of Jesus' words, "Blessed are the pure in heart for they shall see God," (Matt 5:8—unless otherwise noted all references in this chapter are CEB), my memory took me back to Mount Nahum. In 2011 we travelled to Jerusalem to visit one of my wife's more enduring school friends. We were lovers of Jesus. They were committed to observe Torah. A friendship had survived, and even flourished, despite the tyranny of distance. These friends were the most generous of hosts and took

1. Gorman, *Participating in Christ*, 3–7.

2. Williams, *The Wound of Knowledge*, 14.

a day out to travel to Galilee on a Sunday. Access to the tourist facilities were closed, but the view of Lake Galilee was stunning on this blue-sky occasion. It was easy to imagine Jesus sitting and teaching, as Matthew depicts, with a crowd attentive in the natural amphitheater that receded away. Breathtaking beauty must have been a distraction to staying on script.

At this point, Matthew isn't simply conveying a wonderful speech by this new Moses. The one who will "save His people from their sins" (Matt 1:21) is also the one driven to Egypt as a political refugee, the one who was hunted down by opponents to death on a Roman cross. Matthew has presented Jesus as issuing a challenge to all powers, all authorities, and to any and every evil with these words: "change your hearts and lives! Here comes the kingdom of heaven" (Matt 4:17).

In this teacher's Gospel,[3] the narrative we find prior to the Beatitudes, is of Jesus at the center of suffering. We are told "people brought to Him all those who had various kinds of diseases, those in pain, those possessed by demons, those with epilepsy, and those who were paralyzed, and he healed them" (Matt 4:24). What Jesus will teach his disciples, and us today, comes from the incarnation of God in the suffering of the world. Such incarnation will embrace the crucifixion, break the power of death through resurrection, and set free the joy and comforting presence of the Spirit to the end of the age. At the end of my day, was I ready to hear Jesus words, "Blessed are the pure in heart"?

I enjoyed a restful sleep. With breakfast, showering, and conversations about the day soon behind, the radio was waiting for me as I started my vehicle. Today's news was no better than yesterday's! The focus for commentary this morning was domestic violence. What is it that inspires such irritable disrespect among lovers? These experts were confessing their impotence. There was agreement that unlimited government funding would not achieve the personal transformation required for lasting change. Perhaps sustained, across-the-board education for our children was the only hope?

I was thinking "pure in heart" now. Moral education or transformational change? What was Jesus up to, seated on that mountain? The story suggests he was addressing both his close disciples and the large crowd gathered (Matt 5:1). My reflection merged into the steady encounters of a general practice day. Alcohol excess featured heavily in the suffering of my first patient. She lives in a mobile home "resort" where alcohol-fueled

3. See Minear, *Matthew*.

public nuisance has grown in prevalence during shutdown and isolation in the community. Apparently, our society is consuming 20 percent more alcohol during the COVID-19 pandemic.

As the morning unfolded, I was moving from reinforcing the care of chronic disease (somewhat out of focus because of general community anxiety), to negotiating access for acute care and then serious mental health challenges such as adolescent bullying, family grief, family conflict, and depression. Was moral education or counseling going to make this world a better place? I had not become despondent, but I was sensing an agreement with Curt Thompson, who observes, "When our hearts remain a closed system, they tend toward a greater state of chaos and disconnection."[4] This is the story of pandemic crisis, but it is also the background radiation of our lives.

The biblical story out of which Christians live is attentive to our hearts. Jeremiah expresses a prophetic angst when he says, "The heart is deceitful above all things and beyond cure" (Jer 17:9 NIV). He goes on, " I the Lord probe the heart" (Jer 17:10). Can any of us stand tall against such scrutiny? Psalm 24 comes from another angle: The earth is the Lord's. This is the poetry of King David. David knows it is only a "fool who says in his heart there is no God" (Ps 53:1 NIV). He knows about "sinful folly" (Ps 38:5 NIV), he knows he should "muzzle" (Ps 39:1 NIV) his tendency to sin, but he also senses we are all the "apple of God's eye" (Ps 17:8 NIV), and that "God's anger lasts only for a moment, but His love for a lifetime" (Ps 30:5 NIV). So David can say in Psalm 24:34, "Who may stand in His holy place? He who has clean hands and a pure heart." Here is someone who knows what it takes, but with repeated failure (particularly in his famous affair with Bathsheba), David will finally plead for God's mercy to "create in me a clean heart and renew a steadfast spirit within me" (Ps 51:10 NIV).

Matthew continues this ongoing story line about our hearts. After identifying Jesus as the coming Savior (Matt 1:21), John the Baptizer starts the call for change in our hearts (Matt 3:13), and Jesus runs with it (Matt 4:17), stating the obvious: "Healthy people don't need a doctor, but sick people do" (Matt 9:12). Now we are talking. Not only do we need pulse and blood pressure checks. Not only ECGs, stress echocardiograms and angiograms, but as sinners, we need Jesus in order to become pure in heart. For Matthew, the prognosis without Jesus is bleak. During COVID-19 we have learned the rhythms of hygiene to stay clear of the virus. Social distancing,

4. Thompson, *Anatomy of the Soul*, 170.

face masks, and hand washing with soap. Yet at any moment in history, Jesus probes our perplexity: "Don't you understand yet? Don't you know that everything that goes into the mouth enters the stomach and goes out into the sewer? But what comes out of the mouth comes from the heart. And that is what contaminates a person in God's sight. Out of the heart come evil thoughts, murders, adultery, sexual sins, thefts, false testimonies, and insults" (Matt 15:16–19).

In crisis, what is in our hearts moves onto our sleeves as fear. So, what is this pure heart our teacher is pointing toward? Henri Nouwen observes, "Our wounds, whether visible or hidden, are too deep for us to offer each other a place totally free from fear."[5] Our human condition is puzzling.

One of the desert fathers, Evagrius, gathered the meditations of his desert friends as they considered how sin impacts our hearts. He describes "eight deadly thoughts."[6] These monks were motivated to follow Christ in the words of St. Anthony: "Our life and our death is with our neighbor. If we win our brother, we win God. If we cause our brother (or sister) to stumble, we have sinned against Christ."[7] The deadly thoughts were recognized as resulting in anxiety, driven actions, and desires around basic human and relational needs. Sins are the desires and actions that develop when we become disconnected from the love of God. Coming from a perspective that the Christian life is a "race to be run" (2 Tim 4:17), a life requiring preparation, discipline, and the capacity to help our neighbor, their thinking crystallized.

The Eight Deadly Thoughts

The first territory of sin arises around food security anxieties. Fast food advertisers love these concerns. The big sins stand out—gluttony, waste, a failure to share, and perhaps worse, the lack of thankfulness for our daily bread. Sexual lust was number two. We all struggle with sexual sin. We mostly keep these anxieties under the covers. The NSW police commissioner worked hard to keep a straight face when he complained about clearing a traffic jam outside of Sydney's last brothel to remain open prior to the COVID-19 shutdown. Anxieties, selfish desires around almost anything, but especially money, fits under the umbrella of greed. Toilet paper somehow became the

5. Nouwen, *In the House of the Lord*, 23.
6. Allen, *Spiritual Theology*, 64–79.
7. Williams, *Where God Happens*, 9.

icon of greed during the COVID-19 pandemic. Sin is easy when our focus for life does not cultivate the love of God.

Number four was sadness. Here the thinking is about "the sins of unrealistic fantasies of how much greater we might have become."[8] This is the space of the lackluster, frustrations, disappointment, and failure. In this part of life, number five, the emotion of anger with all its bitterness may emerge. Sin also arises in the context of suppressed anger, the unwillingness to let go of the emotion of being sinned against.

Deadly thought six was termed sloth by Pope Gregory; however, the desert fathers had in mind the thoughts of boredom and apathy that lead to despair. While despair and the "dark night of the soul"[9] are often part of the spiritual journey in life,[10] the anxiety of boredom is often at the root of new sins. My grandmother used to love quoting the proverb, "Satan finds mischief for idle hands to do." Number seven is vainglory. These deadly thoughts arise when we notice our maturity and growth in Christ, and want others to notice it. Am I good enough? Have I prayed enough? Am I as Christlike as my friends?

The final territory of deadly thoughts is pride. Our inherent sense of self-worth, and our desire for self-realization, are God-given.[11] Nevertheless, thinking too highly of ourselves scatters us in many dangerous directions. If we are blind to our own pride, there are many role models to catch our attention. We despair when these sins cause us to fall. Allen summarizes this, "The passions that the eight deadly thoughts arouse, inhibit the work of the Holy Spirit in our lives, and keep us from loving God and our neighbor."[12] So what makes the difference? How does the teaching, the cross, and resurrection of Jesus, the baptism of the Holy Spirit sustain and transform our hearts? How can we measure the fruit of "seeing God" (Matt 11:19, 23–26)?

It is not every day a patient asks, "Will you share Jesus with my husband the next time he visits you? He needs a man to tell him the good news." This telehealth consultation was to arrange prescriptions for his arthritis condition. Two years ago, she had a bout of pneumonia. She was facing a respiratory distress death in intensive care, like many during our

8. Allen, *Spiritual Theology*, 72.

9. St. John of the Cross.

10. Allen, *Spiritual Theology*, 75.

11. Allen, *Spiritual Theology*, 77.

12. Allen, *Spiritual Theology*, 78.

pandemic. Her friends were praying for God's mercy and healing. She told me she felt like she was drowning at the bottom of a swimming pool when, all of a sudden, the water started to swirl. The power in the water was lifting her up. As she surfaced, she knew she would live and indeed told anyone who would listen, including her husband, of her miracle. With this shared knowledge, I sensed an opportunity to check in with her about COVID-19. As it transpired, she was more concerned about her husband's health and well-being.

Segundo Galilea suggests that "Jesus Himself is the incarnation of the Beatitudes. Lived and proclaimed by Him, they become the spiritual values of a Kingdom that is primarily Jesus Himself."[13] Our gospel is a comprehensive engagement with this statement. Jesus is the true Son of God, the true Israelite, who is pure in heart, the One who offers the world extraordinary mercy through His sacrifice. As the resurrected Messiah emerging from the lockdown of his tomb, he reengages with the disciples. They had self-quarantined in the expectation of political harassment. In Matthew's story (Matt 28:1-10), two women—both named Mary—with a mixture of courage and fear are present at the tomb on resurrection morning. The sight of an angel rolling away the entrance stone, and then sitting on it, must have disturbed their implicit understanding of reality. The terrified guards began shaking and then assumed the posture of the dead. This was not a horror movie. The angelic conversation alerted the women that the "eucatastrophe"[14] of crucifixion has now issued into resurrection. They accept the offer of inspecting the now empty grave, and with fear running into excitement, hurry off to tell the disciple-band. Whatever we assumed about being pure in heart, has now been turned on its head. The disciples grabbed Jesus' feet as he greeted them a short time later. How do you respond to this climactic event in world history? Can you imagine encountering the resurrected Jesus?

Gospel storytellers, Matthew and Mark, somehow keep the lid on this death-defying event (Matt 28; Mark 16:18). Like the disciples, we should be afraid. But unexpectedly, from this healing fault-line in human history, Jesus invites "all my brothers and sisters" to meet him back in Galilee (Matt 28:10). All that Jesus has taught on the mountain, all that has been demonstrated through healing acts, exorcisms, and attentiveness to the least of these will be remembered through the reality of resurrection. A fake media campaign emerges as the scared-to-death soldiers report to the authorities.

13. Galilea, *The Way of Living Faith*, 49.

14. Tolkien, *On Fairy Stories* in Flieger and Anderson, 75.

Its tweets are regularly forwarded on. As hearers of the story, our calling is to go back to Galilee, baptized in the Holy Spirit (Matt 3:11) to take up the cross daily (Matt 26:34). In the time of crisis, it will be hearing the words of Jesus, the encouragement to be pure in heart, now associated with the resurrected Messiah, that will be our hope!

Being both present to Jesus and listening to his teaching will require three steps in our spiritual pilgrimage: practices, participation, and productivity.

Practices

Engaging with people around practices for good health, such as healthy eating, modest alcohol consumption, and undertaking regular exercise, is to encourage holistic health benefits. Managing the chronic disease risk factors created by hypertension, diabetes, and so forth also requires good rhythms. During a crisis, health rhythms and practices remain foundational to good health.

As the curve of COVID-19 infection flattens, a second wave of mental health distress is emerging. Previously managed fears now escape to irritability, jaded decision-making, violence, and alcohol misuse. "Tony's" body is worn down by heavy laboring work. He was unemployed and drinking too much before the pandemic. He is haunted by the murder of his eldest brother, shot through the front door of the home when he was still a boy. The trauma lives with him. Social stress and COVID-19 saw "Tony" yelling down the phone line as he became overwhelmed with his stressors. The narrative of distress is kaleidoscopic. Also, being present to an experienced pastor openly weeping and now depressed because of his distress for the people of God, stripped of the fellowship of the Spirit during lockdown, is confronting. Christian fellowship is a sustaining practice for all who are in-Christ.

I am suggesting that hearing Matthew's narrative in the presence of the living resurrected Jesus and the comfort of the Spirit quickly alerts us to good practices. As we move beyond the Beatitudes, Jesus' teaching regularly draws attention to practices. Here we find the encouragement to be attentive to the demands of Torah, to practice reconciliation, to be committed to nonviolence and the "suffering of insults," and to practice the "law of love" (Matt 5:17–48). Matthew's Jesus is keen to show that living the Beatitudes is a challenge to hypocrisy in religious observance, showy prayer practices, self-promoting fasting, and hypocrisy in service (Matt 6:5–24).

This global pandemic has seen widespread lockdowns and self-isolation at home to restrain this evil contagion. While our home has spacious surrounds, the busyness of life has led us to neglect its maintenance and underdevelop its potential. Like so many, we unexpectedly found ourselves with time to prune branches, dig the soil, and remove weeds and roots so as to create garden beds for planting vegetables and fruit trees. Without these sweaty practices, the land stays quietly unproductive. Now we can expect a future good harvest. What are the practices that sustain you in crisis? In the presence of the resurrected Christ, what practices help you to listen for, and see (Matt 13:14–16) the kingdom coming today?

Barclay notes the term *pure in heart* refers to mixed motives and continues, "There are few things in this world that even the best of us do with completely unmixed motives."[15] Practices operate in our lives to help us remain attentive to Jesus' guidance, and to promote the desire to "seek first God's kingdom" (Matt 6:33). This gospel contains many reorientating challenges. Let your yes be yes and your no be no (Matt 5:37); enter the narrow gate (Matt 7:13–14); maintain the preference of mercy over sacrifice (Matt 9:13); become people of faith (Matt 7:14–20); hold childlike trust in Jesus' presence (Matt 18:15); and be a people who forgive (Matt 18:21–23). Tyson helpfully recognizes that *metanoia* (a Greek word we have translated as repentance) is "a forward-looking word . . . a transformed vision, indeed, the transformed vision one receives from God."[16] So practices prepare and maintain the participatory and productive nature of Christian life. Three practices stand out as crisis sustainers.

1. Prayer. I have been nourished and blessed by online prayer during this pandemic. Prayers of lament, prayer in unity, prayer for the world, and prayer for peace. Prayer calls out the surrender of our heart to God in love. Delio guides us in these words, "The Spirit urges those in whom the Spirit dwells to pray with a pure heart and with all the diversity and richness that such prayer implies."[17]
2. Entering the story of Scripture, Matthew is our guide to see the living Beatitudes among us. The Scriptures are God's story to us with the

15. Barclay, *Gospel of Matthew*, 101–3.
16. Tyson, *Returning to Reality*, 197.
17. Delio, *Franciscan Prayer*, 9.

cross as "God's signature,"[18] the guarantee of his self-giving love, "shed abroad in our hearts" (Rom 5:5). This word nourishes us for love. It is a word that promises if we love Jesus, we will keep his commands (John 14:15), the blessing of a pure heart. We need intentionally to engage and reengage with Scripture. If we don't know the story, it is unlikely to be sustaining in crisis. As Allen puts it, "This is probably why spirituality in general, in spite of its initial appeal, fails us. When the chips are down, vagueness about what we believe is not an asset."[19]

3. Fellowship. The way of living the Beatitudes draws us inevitably into the gathering of communities centered in Christ. Crises can be inherently challenging to fellowship practices. In times of self-isolation, we need the imaginative fire of the Spirit to maintain fellowship. For many, technology platforms such as Zoom, WhatsApp, etc. have proved a game-changer. Pastoral care systems are now sustained through technology. While we have accepted adjustment to virtual community, the way ahead is not so clear. What are the solutions to long-term pressures against community? Jesus promises to be always with the gathering of two or three (Matt 18:20).

In the mix are "care armies," hospitality practices such as preparing meals for families escaping domestic violence, food hampers for poor families, families without work income, and overseas students with no ongoing access to casual jobs. Pohl warns us, "In the history of Christian monasticism, tensions accompanied every attempt to reconcile spiritual life with the reception of guests."[20] To be pure in heart is to keep practices of community and hospitality alive in times of crisis. How connected to a community are you?

Participation

Practices contribute to our readiness to participate in the life of the kingdom before, during, and after times of crisis. They prepare the way we enter into the life of the Beatitudes embodied in Jesus. The teaching of Jesus becomes thick, rich, and holds life-giving power, because of the crucifixion and resurrection of Emmanuel (Matt 1:23). Our living teacher is "with us to the end

18. Ernst Kasemann, cited in Gorman, *Participating in Christ*, 97.

19. Allen, *Spiritual Theology*, 159.

20. Pohl, *Making Room*, 139.

of this present age" (Matt 28:20). As we "return to Galilee" (Matt 28:10) we discover the blessed assurance of Jesus ever present with us.

While Matthew only suggests glimpses of the Holy Spirit, the Apostle John describes the Spirit as our comforter (John 14:16). For Matthew, it will be John the Baptizer who confidently asserts "He [Jesus] will baptize you with the Holy Spirit and fire" (Matt 3:11). Matthew probes our human weakness and ambiguity when he reports Jesus' words, "Those who don't pick up their crosses and follow me are not worthy of me. Those who find their lives will lose them, and those who lose their lives because of me will find them" (Matt 10:39).

This Gospel lesson concludes with Jesus commissioning our participation in the Emmanuel-event with a call to "make disciples of all nations, baptizing them in the name of the Father, Son, and Holy Spirit" (Matt 28:19). As the resurrected and ascending Jesus promises to be with us, we are left with the unspoken life of the Spirit in our lives. We are left with what has been termed, "plan be."[21] The "be-attitudes" of Holy Spirited lives.

It will take other gospel storytellers to provide more details about the Spirit mediating the joy of living the Beatitudes. Paul described our participation very clearly in this way, "Thus, I myself no longer live, but the Messiah lives in me, and the life I do now live in the flesh, I live by means of the faithfulness of the Son of God, who loved me by giving himself for me" (Gal 2:20).[22]

In this conversation about the call to be pure in heart in times of crisis, Paul centers his life in the crisis of God, the faithful, self-giving crucifixion love of the messiah Jesus. Paul encountered the living Jesus graphically on the road to Damascus. Everything in the world changed for Paul. Thomas á Kempis understood Paul's witness when he wrote, "Jesus hath many lovers of the kingdom of heaven, but few bearers of the cross."[23] At Galilee then, Jesus invites his disciples to the life of resurrectional cruciformity[24] or cruciform authenticity.[25] To be pure in heart becomes a fully human experience[26] in lives which daily die with Christ and rise with Christ (Rom 6).

21. Andrews, *Plan Be.*

22. Translation by Gorman, *Participating in Christ,* 117.

23. Thomas á Kempis, cited in Green and Stevens, *New Testament Spirituality*, 38.

24. Gorman, *Participating in Christ*, 53–76.

25. N. T. Wright, cited in Gorman, *Participating in Christ*, 33.

26. Gorman, *Participating in Christ*, 75.

Productivity

"Models of spirituality can baptize will-lessness and willfulness in the name of faith."[27] In reflecting through this Beatitude, we are recognizing a spirituality that neither withdraws from crisis nor demands to control outcomes. To be pure at heart is to live out God's self-emptying, self-giving, crucifixional love in resurrection power. Luke Johnson suggests that "Jesus' great threat to sin . . . is in the simple gesture of treating every person as of equal and infinite worth to God."[28] This orientates our productiveness in Christ toward compassionate dignity. E. Stanley Jones recognizes that "the words of Jesus, 'I am the resurrection and the life,' sets the sorrows of life to music and makes the climate note to be joy."[29]

Our narrator works with the teaching material, the practices, the participatory transformation of his Gospel to demonstrate fruit (Matt 12:33–36), to notice a productive harvest (Matt 13:39), to encourage disciples to become healers (Matt 8 and 9), and to motivate disciples to accept the challenge of mission (Matt 10). Jesus teaches productivity. When John the Baptist's disciples approach him with uncertainties about Jesus' messiahship (the one to come), we are given an unexpected bottom line: "Those who were blind are able to see. Those who are crippled are walking. People with skin diseases are cleansed. Those who are deaf now hear. Those who were dead are raised up. The poor have good news proclaimed to them" (Matt 11:2–6).

The outcome for disciples is not dissimilar. Mercy, not sacrifice, will count (Matt 12:7). Service not power-seeking is valued (Matt 20:24–28). The self-righteous fail, but tax collectors and sinners have a good chance to pass (Matt 21:23–32). Indeed, on exam day (the last judgment), Jesus openly identifies the pure in heart, the ones who receive "the kingdom prepared for you" (Matt 25:36–48) as those who have ministered to Jesus himself, "I was hungry and you gave me food to eat, I was thirsty and you gave me a drink. I was a stranger and you welcomed me. I was naked and you gave me clothes to wear. I was in prison and you visited me"(Matt 25:35).

During our current crisis and indeed the history of the world since the eucatastrophe of the Jesus' event, the pure in heart continue to respond to the care of the least. The world has changed and is changing, yet

27. Johnson, *Faith's Freedom*, 115.

28. Johnson, *Faith's Freedom*, 163.

29. Jones, *Christ and Human Suffering*, 250.

the enduring witness of the lives of many is in courageous, loving, selfless service. The productivity of the love of God has been wonderful in every way as this pandemic plays out. Nouwen notices for us: "The great news of the gospel is precisely that God became small and vulnerable, and hence bore fruit among us."[30]

Arguably, the iconic story of the pandemic surrounds Dr. Li Wenliang, an ophthalmologist from the Chinese city of Wuhan, who had the eyes to see the inherent danger in new cases of pneumonia of unknown etiology resulting in death. As a member of the Christian community in this epicenter of the COVID-19 pandemic, Dr. Li sought to warn the world by raising concerns with local officials. His life was taken by the illness he recognized. Soon other Christians, dubbed the "yellow angels,"[31] also became active in Wuhan. Dressing in yellow PPE, they moved onto the streets to hand out masks and gospel tracts. What will your productive response look like in times of crisis? As those who follow the crucified, resurrected Jesus, who teaches and lives the way of the pure in heart, are we ready for the cold dark nights to come? We see God as we are.

30. Nouwen, *In the House*, 41.

31. Wong, "'Angels in yellow.'"

Prayer: Pure in Heart in Time of Crisis —Addressing the Eight Deadly Thoughts

In this day of alarm and fear we sit with brothers and sisters at the feet of Jesus. We see in his face both the scars of the cross and the glory of resurrection life. It is only your grace that can cleanse our hands and purify our hearts.

Lord, you invite us to petition for our daily bread, yet in this fearful time, we have been anxious for our food-security. Have we also hoarded? Have we forgotten to share in the light of all your generosity? Have we doubted your providential care? Indeed, Lord, when did we see you hungry?

[Silence]

Lord, have mercy. Forgive these sins. Restore the joy of your banqueting love.

Lord, you have given the creative and joyful gift of sexual activity for the stewardship of human life and our pleasure. Yet in anxiety about our sexual needs, we have grasped at your gift. We easily objectify the sexuality of our neighbor. We seek our own gratification, and forget your loyal, serving love.

[Silence]

Lord, have mercy. Forgive these sins. Restore the passionate joy of sexuality as your gift.

Lord, out of your abundance, you bless us with all that we need to live well. Yet we confess to being restless consumers. Our desires are consuming us. We are driven to seek more. We are anxious that we are never wealthy enough. Our clutter blinds us to the reality that "You are all we need." When did we meet you in need, Lord?

[Silence]

Lord, have mercy. Forgive our sins. Restore the generosity of a loving heart in us.

Our Lord, we are all "could-have-been champions." We all live with failed dreams of love that "got away." We have had high hopes, only to see them dashed. We confess that in such experiences we have become despondent. We are easily frustrated; we struggle with failures. As we default to sadness, we plead, shine your light through cracks of grace.

Lord have mercy, in good times and bad, strengthen our life in the resurrection power of the Spirit.

[Silence]

Oh, Lord, why is anger so bitter and destructive to relationships? Why is anger, which shuts you out, so "natural" to us? Our anger can evolve to many faces of sin: domestic violence, road rage, unforgiving hearts. And in anger we scapegoat, we can bully and troll our way through life's spaces.

[Silence]

Lord, have mercy. Through your Spirit alive in our hearts, help us to live lives of love. This is all that matters.

Lord, we sense an amazing privilege in your call to partnership in creation-care and love of neighbor. Often our response is impacted by boredom, a reluctance to remain involved, and despair. Life can seem too difficult. Remind us you look into the eyes of our hearts.

[Silence]

Lord, have mercy. Forgive our sins. Call us again to good-spirited stewardship.

Lord, we so easily turn from humility to self-promotion. We yearn to be congratulated for faithfulness in Jesus. As we follow in his steps, keep us at the point of grace. In-Christ, we are all on equal footing. Forgive us for manipulating our experience of your love to gain recognition, to seek important positions, and to cultivate a spirit of entitlement against the work of sustaining the least of our—and your—brothers and sisters.

[Silence]

The cross is the signature of your love. Lord have mercy, transform your people to the character of cross-shaped lives.

It feels easy not to honor you as Lord, when pride is central in our lives. Pride leads to sin in so many ways. Break down our arrogance, our unwillingness to be teachable. Call out our desires to lord it over others, to expect to be loved and served. Expose all the ways we sense we are important to the detriment of others.

[Silence]

Lord, have mercy. Lead us back to Jesus, who faithfully makes himself of no reputation, so that we are saved by grace alone.

Blessed are the peacemakers,
for they will be called children of God.

Lord, you say to us:

"My peace I leave with you; my peace I give to you.

I do not give to you as the world gives.

Do not let your hearts be troubled, and do not let them be afraid" (John 14:27 NRSV). It is your peace, not the peace the world gives, that we so need amid this pandemic crisis. You invite us to take your peace into our being,

and to become your peacemakers in the interpersonal and group settings in which you place us,

encouraging cooperation and self-giving rather than competition and contest.

Offering your way of peace becomes another mark of our kingdom character.

7

Guides for the Soul

Christopher Brown

Encountering the Troubled Soul

In chapter 1, mention is made of a thirty-eight-year-old man, Bob, who has been impacted by the upheaval of the pandemic. He becomes the focus of a faith-based men's group, who initially engage with him over his surprise at his anger at failing to secure a job opening earlier that evening.

In this chapter, I offer an illustration of how such a group might provide guidance and support to each other, and to troubled pilgrims through a time of crisis.[1] I resonate strongly with Tim McCowan in chapter 7, "Stay with Me." He pointed to how Jesus would release the healing power of the Spirit already present in the situation, rather than introducing something external and new. Paul Mercer, in chapter 8, "In-Christ, in Crisis," offers a timely warning. He cites Henri Nouwen, who observes: "Our wounds, whether visible or hidden, are too deep for us to offer each other a place totally free from fear."[2] When engaging with an individual's experience (my story), it is important to acknowledge such an encounter occurs in the context of relationships (our story), and within an even greater story (the God story). It is the presence of the Spirit, who enables such an engagement.

1. A constructed narrative is used because in the guiding of the soul, pilgrim experiences and accounts are held in confidential and sacred trust.

2. Nouwen, *In the House*, 23.

The Group

Before engaging with Bob's experience of being accompanied and guided, we meet the men of this group who have experienced the Spirit's call to the sacred task of guiding troubled souls through and beyond the pandemic. These ordinary, everyday men, some from the schools of "hard knocks," have responded to the prophetic imperative of looking beyond merely enduring a crisis to seeking a changing relationship with both God and their neighbor. They acknowledge, from their experiential knowing and prayerful theological reflection, how this pandemic offers a catalyst for renewed kingdom-citizenship and participation amid societal upheaval in ways reflective of the kingdom of heaven. Jesus' Sermon on the Mount, and particularly his Beatitudes, were foremost in their reflections, reshaping them through what some call a "living exegesis."

Though impacted in different ways by the pandemic crisis, these men noticed common threads weaving through their experiences. Some saw how their default responses to challenging circumstances could quickly escalate. This was described by one member as "the escalation of my shadowy defaults!" Their spirits were unsettled and anxious. New tasks were foisted upon them, requiring creativity and adaptation, such as working from home, helping with home schooling, taking more responsibility for children and elderly relatives. There were financial insecurities and worries about the future, including that of lack of jobs.

As part of a local church, they had come together through Joe and Mark's initiative of a "beer and Bible" group. Turned upside-down by the pandemic, their group became a lifeline. They gave up the "beer" focus, took more to Scripture, prayer, and supportive conversations, and committed to meet weekly via Zoom. Growing in awareness of the Spirit's touch in their formation, they began to discover the sacred rhythms and flows underlying their everyday human experiences. Praying for the kingdom to be manifest on earth during this crisis took a central place alongside St. Patrick's prayer, that Christ be "within and without me, lowly and meek, yet all-powerful, be in the heart of each to whom I speak; in the mouth of each who speaks unto me." Conversations were held in confidence and sacred trust. Jesus' Sermon on the Mount and the Beatitudes were forefront.

The practice of silent prayer was gradually introduced, given one member's claim that "men needed to be in silence." Their earlier practice of back-and-forth conversations gave way to listening to men's experiences and struggles, one at a time. They pulled back from judging and analyzing, from advice-giving, and from commenting on one another's experiences. It was Jesus' Beatitudinal presence they sought to reflect and embody. Aware that they were all poor in spirit, they opened their hearts to the Spirit's giftings of mercy, transparency of heart, clarity of discernment, peacemaking, along with divine strength in the face of opposition. Agape love occupied them.

Human experience, especially that impacted and amplified by the pandemic, was considered as a site of encounter with the Divine. Active dialogue developed between experience and Scripture, and between experience and the *Living Word*. Encountering Jesus as *Friend, Redeemer, Reconciler, Healer*, and *Lord* amid challenging human experiences, became, for these men, the cauldron for change! Enlivened by the Spirit, their character became shaped in the spirit of the Beatitudes for renewed kingdom citizenship, and for being guides to the troubled soul. Prayer was often heart-wrenching as the pandemic continued to open up cracks within and around them. As men, co-existing in a culture of rough speaking, they took to heart one member's prayer meditation, suggesting the drenching of each spoken word in grace and compassion, and tempering each encounter with truth and clarity and "seasoned with salt" (Col 4:6 TPT).

The night of Bob's visit was the first group meeting after the easing of the lockdown. So they were meeting at Joe's.

Bob's Experience

Bob has lost his job, his work identity, and the companionship of his colleagues due to the pandemic shutdown. He had just visited a former colleague hoping he might know of an job opening. It was early evening and, driving away, his first thought was of meeting some old workmates at the pub and drowning his sorrows. But driving past Joe's house, he remembered that the men's group, which he occasionally attends, would be meeting. Realizing that his pub mates would try to jolly him up with more rounds of beer, and how that would not augur well for a good start of the next morning home schooling his ten-year-old daughter, he did a u-turn.

Bob entered Joe's sitting room just as one of the men was lighting the meeting-candle and reminding the group of Christ's presence. Bob was glad that the men would hold ten minutes of silent prayer at the beginning of their meeting. This practice offered him time to settle his jangled nerves and to push against the mixture of shame and anger that were coursing through his body. Then, as the silence broke, Joe turned to him, opened out his arms, and said: "Welcome Bob, any luck on the job front?"

"No luck there, mate. Just another dead-end!" "Dead end," Bob thought, was a good descriptor. But it didn't settle his anger or shame. As he sat amid these good and committed friends, it was a sadness that had joined these other emotions.

Joe waited for a few moments until Bob looked up in his direction. "Just another dead-end," he repeated. "What's it like for you in that place, Bob?"

Bob glanced around the room seeking out the faces of his friends. He was surprised that some eyes were moist and that there was genuine concern for his well-being.

"When I left Mick's place, I thought my jeep wasn't going to start, so I banged my hand on the steering wheel. It shook me a bit realizing how angry I was. But as I got going, I realized there was more down there." Bob was pointing to his lower stomach. "I was angry, but I was also ashamed." Bob paused. "I've put a lot into providing for my family; in fact, I've worked my butt off. So losing my job was like losing everything. And why would I even say that? And as I sit with you guys spilling my guts, this thing in my stomach is starting to move. A minute ago, there was anger and shame. Now what's coming in their place is sadness: like a lot of sadness. And as it comes, I just get this thought that it's about more than just losing a job!"

"A lot of sadness, that's more than about losing a job," said Joe. "Can we all just sit with you awhile in that place, Bob?"

It was Bob who broke the two-minute silence. "An odd thought has come. It's like I'm totally bereft."

The murmur around the room indicated that the word *bereft* had struck a chord and resonated in the hearts of these men. Most had followed Bob's inward trajectory as it began with anger, moved to shame, to sadness, to something that was more than losing a job, and then to "bereft." Bob had named something familiar. Bob and this company of men had moved onto holy ground. A doorway to the soul was ajar through which the Divine had squeezed. The task of Joe and these men was to encourage Bob in attending prayerfully to what continued to unfold before him. After all, had not these same men committed to praying, especially during this time of the pandemic, "your kingdom come, your will be done, on earth as in heaven"?

"Totally Bereft"

In the safe, non-judgmental, and confidential space of interpersonal solidarity that these men along with the Spirit offered, Bob notices an inner shift from anger to shame and then to a pang of deep sadness. Encouraged to stay attentive to what emerges for him, Bob finds himself "totally bereft"! The responding murmur of those present indicated that Bob's experience had touched receptive hearts. Nestling amid such murmurs, the ever-present Holy Spirit gathers these heart stirrings into a community of intention and trust, who come alongside Bob as his interior doorway opens into the deeper reaches of his soul. With their spirits enlivened, seven men stand with Bob at the edge of an unfolding mystery.

> The phrase "totally bereft,"
> settles on receptive hearts;
> while momentarily resting
> upon the Spirit's open palm.
> There it exchanged for a master key
> which enlivens spirits
> and opens soul-shaped locks
> from the inside.

Bob's description of being "totally bereft" was the moment in which heartfelt solidarity developed between Bob and the other men. The Holy Spirit had enlivened Bob's spirit to enable him to engage with and be fully attentive to what was emerging in front of him. He then spoke of being dropped into a "new world" and being at a loss in knowing how to respond. He began to notice that the experience of "bereft" was a feeling of powerlessness and of loss of control in most areas of his life. It was, he said, "like living in a house I didn't know," and feeling ashamed that he was losing his momentum. It is Joe to whom the group looks to guide Bob further. Their conversation continues.

Joe: Bob, you mentioned your experience of being bereft was like living in an unknown house, and a feeling of shame at losing your momentum. If you were able to look at yourself in that house, I wonder what you might notice.

Bob: (*Shuffles around in his chair, finds a comfortable spot and closes his eyes.*) It's almost completely dark inside, and the house is very unstable. I'm grabbing on to things, trying to get my balance, but they tend to break and fall away. It's now like I've left a whole lot of repairs undone but can't find the tools to fix them. That's odd, Joe, because in real life, my workshop is all neat and my tools well organized. But not here!

Bob has the image of a collapsing house and of not being able to find his tools to fix it. Often men like Bob, especially those whose focus has been the external world with little attention to their interior, are still to learn the more vibrant and revealing language of the soul. That in no way inhibits the Spirit! The door to the soul is open. With Bob's spirit enlivened, the Spirit can prompt imagery, active imagination, metaphor, parable, as well as words for the discoveries and revelations of his soul. The Spirit has also inducted some of the men in these gently oblique and non-direct ways.

Joe: As you notice the instability, the difficulty you have in maintaining your balance, and you can't find your tools to do the repairs, what happens next?

Bob: A window, which has just shattered, draws my attention. Through the broken glass, I can see outside. Everything is upside-down and in a real mess. There is also an ominous dark cloud. Even though things are unstable inside of the house, fear—even dread—accompanies the thought of going outside.

Joe: Bob, see if you can stay with the fear, even the dread of going outside.

Bob: (*Has become restless and unsettled in his chair.*) I'm stuck. I can't move. Not that I necessarily want to move. But I don't like this feeling of being stuck. It's not like me to be stuck. I usually pride myself in making things happen. But in here, in this collapsing house, without being able to find my tools, I now feel like I couldn't even get out of a paper bag!

Joe: I wonder, Bob, if you could observe this person of you: the person who usually can make things happen, but now is stuck?

Bob: (*Looking unsure.*) I would, but he's all jittery, and that makes me feel jittery as well. It's like when I was a kid, and there was a lot of upset and conflict. I remember saying to God I needed someone who could explain things.

Joe: And how did God respond?

Bob: He sent my grandfather, and I just sat close by him. I can't remember all he said, except not to be afraid, but I know I felt safe and less jittery.

Joe: What do you notice about your grandfather as you sit close to him?

Bob: He's calm even in a crisis. He's a man of faith who used to say his anchor in any storm was God. During that family crisis, he was my anchor. For a moment, it seemed like he had come to sit with me in this collapsing house, but now he has gone, and I know he's with God. (*Bob was becoming teary.*)

At this point, there was a slight stirring among some of the men. Bob's account had prompted a stirring in their souls. Their experiential knowing, including their pain, was being wordlessly offered as the Spirit gathers it up, bringing these men, along with their lived and prayed-over experiences, into deeper solidarity with Bob.

Joe: What is the gift of your grandfather, Bob, amid the collapsing house?

Bob: It was the seat—that place of calm amid the storm—that he guided me to. He left me the source of his calm and peace as well.

Joe: From that seat, from that place of calm anchored in God, what do you see now?

Bob: There is a sizeable cloud-like shape in front of me, blocking my vision.

Joe: What do you notice if you look directly at it; like eyeball it?

Bob: It shrinks a bit, and I seem prompted to ask its name! It says: "I'm *Fear*!"

In what follows, Bob is enabled to unmask fear and the over-protective role it has been playing in his life. Along with shame and doubt, fear has stood in the way of him exploring the cellar of the collapsing house: a basement he hardly knew was there. *Fear* warns him it is too dangerous, even a matter of life and death! And yet, he finds the courage to explore it.

Joe: (*Speaking gently.*) What are you noticing now as you explore that cellar, Bob?

Bob: (*A tear has formed in the corner of Bob's eye.*) I do know some of what's down there in the cellar. Yes, there is *Fear*, *Shame*, and *Doubt*. And in many ways, as *Fear* intimated, they have sought to protect me. But right now, what's pressing in on me is the distressing realization that I haven't kept faith with something planted deep within me.

Joe: That you haven't kept faith with something planted within you?

Bob: (*Both Bob and Joe sit together through a long silence. Bob reaches for a tissue, drops his head, and closes his eyes. When he breaks the silence, he speaks in a whisper, just loud enough for Joe to hear.*) You know, Joe, when I acknowledged—confessed—not keeping faith, I was guided back to the seat of calm. There was a voice, similar to my grandfather's, saying: "Don't be afraid, Bob." There was no condemnation in that voice. There was forgiveness. It was like being welcomed into a safe and trustworthy place. My grandfather's seat is down in that cellar. Invited to sit there, I'm conscious of an *invisible presence*, like one who had come alongside to listen to the deepest cries of my heart. It's like a cry that spans my life until now. These cries seem to cross the span of my life from childhood up until now. Then follow the things that have caused me anxiety over the past three months. There are images associated with the pandemic; images of unemployed people queuing for job-seeker and job-keeper benefits; images of businesses with "closed" signs on the doors; images of graphs of infections and daily deaths; images of mass burials; images highlighting dichotomies among rich and poor; and, much more. In the face of all of that comes the feeling I mentioned right at the beginning, Joe, of being totally bereft. And there is so much sorrow! (*Bob paused and began to look weary.*) And then all was silent. It was as if my invisible accompanier had drawn me into a silence—a safe, welcoming, and restoring silence—like I hadn't known before.

Joe: Amid the enormity of this, Bob, you experience the accompaniment of an *invisible presence*! Though there is that feeling of being "totally bereft," you are brought to that place of silence, peace, and calm.

Bob: You know, Joe, my grandfather loved the Psalms. It's strange, but the words that come are: "Why my soul are you downcast, why so disquieted within me?" (Ps 43:5). Fancy remembering that! But that's what it is! It's about the upheaval of my soul. There are essential parts of me in the basement of my life with which I have not kept faith. I just distract myself. I get my toolbox from my neatly organized workshop, lose myself in work, or have a drink with a mate, or go for a mountain bike ride with my son. But then comes the lockdown. With less of those external things to distract me, the cast-down nature and disquiet of my soul just bubbles up. Until now, bubbling has been unacknowledged or unknown. (*Bob looks up.*) Joe, could it be that I've been seeking to gain the whole world, yet putting my soul in danger? (Matt 16:26.)

Joe: Do you remember what you experienced before with that voice not unlike your grandfather's, encouraging you not to be afraid? You said there was no condemnation in that voice. Instead, there was forgiveness. You spoke of being welcomed into a safe and solid place. The cellar door, the doorway to the basement of your soul, opens. The *invisible one*, the Holy Spirit, accompanies you. There is a divine invitation to explore and acknowledge the riches, the treasure, and the images of Christ that God has planted there for God's glory.

Bob: (*After a long pause.*) It's coming clear. I now have somewhere to go, (*adding with a smile*) even without that job and in the midst of this pandemic! I need more time on my grandfather's seat in my basement to get God's help with my soul! I think I'm done for tonight, friends! Thanks so much for all that, Joe and the rest of you guys.

Joe: And thank you, Bob, and thanks be to God.

Witnesses to Movements of the Spirit

Called to engage deeply with each other and with those in the world around them, these humble men have witnessed a life-giving and soulful movement in the life of this pilgrim. The movements in which they have participated are those prompted by the Spirit. These are foundational movements initially prompted by crisis. Their impact is profound, involving soul explorations, awakenings, revelations, encounters with the Divine, and a renewal of kingdom citizenship. These movements are also prophetic, culminating in changing relationships with both God and neighbor. Their grace will overflow into other areas of Bob's life and beyond, as it will be for each person present. Whether a pilgrim, a guide, or a witness, being party to life-giving encounters between the Spirit and the soul, leaves no one unchanged!

Reflection

My life must be Christ's broken bread,
My love his outpoured wine,
A cup o'erfilled, a table spread
Beneath his name and sign.
That other souls, refreshed and fed,
May share his life through mine. (Albert Osborne)[3]

How might this be a prayer for you as you ponder companioning troubled pilgrims on their journey of life and faith in the context of a global crisis?

3. Osborne, "My life must be."

Blessed are those who are
persecuted for righteousness' sake,
for theirs is the kingdom of heaven.

Lord, you offer us no illusions for our kingdom citizenship.

Rather you animate us with the courage and the mettle we need to experience persecution for your sake and the sake of the kingdom (Matt 5:3–10).

Above all,

you offer us hope and your presence in circumstances of upheaval and crisis,

so that we can walk in the footsteps of your prophets, embody and reflect your way, and anticipate the fullness of new life that is to come.

8

In the World and Not Afraid

With Inspiration from Our Ancient Forebears

CHARLES RINGMA

Introduction

DESPITE ALL THE PROMISES of prosperity and living the dream of a good life, many in contemporary society live with persistent anxieties. Many of these have to do with changes in our society due to technological innovation, issues relating to our fragile planet, threats to regular employment, the challenge of living in our surveillance society, and the shifting of the geo-political plates leading to emerging new empires.

There are, of course, anxiety-producing factors that are much closer to home. Family dysfunctionality. Ill health. Loss of loved ones. The list is endless but is one that highlights the nature of human fragility. This fragility has been exacerbated by the COVID-19 global health crisis. A crisis that demonstrates the interdependent nature of our world for both good and ill. And a crisis that is testing our health-systems, our economics, our social structures, and our forms of governance. It is testing all of us in terms of adjusting to social isolation and our concerns as to what a new normal might look like. And it has impacted those who have lost jobs and incomes. And in particular, the poor have been dealt a cruel blow. But crises are not new. Every so often a major crisis comes our way. But in some countries, crises are a regular part of life—typhoons, earthquakes, civil wars, and military coups. And there is the reality of grinding poverty for many.

A crisis in society is also a crisis for the church. And the challenge is not only how can the church survive in such a time? The challenge is also how can the faith community respond with practical care? And the underlying challenge is what can we learn about ourselves and others in these circumstances; what change should we anticipate and work towards; and what may God be indirectly saying in these circumstances?

In this chapter, I seek to demonstrate that the church in its 2,000-year journey has always had to face difficulties. Some of these were internal and of its own making, such as doctrinal splits, misuse of power, and internal spiritual decay. But the church has also had to face the headwinds of external factors that have threatened its very existence. These have included wars, famines, pandemics, natural disasters, as well as persecutions.

While the theme of persecution and the promised blessedness is the Beatitude that frames this chapter, the Greek term for persecution also means "to hasten," "to press on," "to strive for," and "to aspire to." Thus, while *pressed upon* by one's persecutors, the persecuted ones *aspire to* their deliverance into the kingdom of heaven. And of course, it is not only persecution that can press in upon us: so can a pandemic and other disasters. In the midst of these calamities, the Beatitude suggests that we are not simply helpless and passive victims. We aspire to seeing redemption and solutions.

In tackling these complex matters in this chapter, I seek to do two things: one, to demonstrate the various responses that the church has made in times of difficulty; and two, to engage the wisdom of the church's forebears about positive and creative responses they made in the face of crises and difficulties. But first, some ancient voices of lament.

Hearing the Voices of Grief and Pain

Unlike those living in the West, who often only hear the voice of blessing and a gospel of prosperity, many of our forebears and those presently living in the Majority world have been shaped by a different gospel. That gospel is not, "Christ has suffered for you therefore you will never have to suffer." Rather it is, "The salvation of Christ draws you into identification with Christ, and therefore, you are called to live like him." Clearly this involves both suffering and service. And since the incarnation—the coming of Christ into the world as one of us—is a core reality, so we too, are called to be part of our neighborhoods and our world.

St. Augustine speaks about life's difficulties. He cries out: "Is not life on earth a trial?" And continues: "because adversity itself is a hard thing, lest it shatter endurance, is not the life of man and woman upon earth all trial?" He goes on to say that none of us "wishes for troubles and difficulties," but we are called "to endure" them. In this process Augustine acknowledges that he gets "wounded" and pleads with God the physician to heal him.[1]

St. John Chrysostom gives us advice regarding how to respond in times of difficulty. He notes: "Whether it be loss of property, or infirmity of the body, or insult, or false accusation or any other form of evil incident to humankind," we are to respond like Job—"the Lord gave, the Lord has taken away . . . blessed be the name of the Lord forever." Chrysostom goes on: "If we practice this spiritual wisdom, we will never experience any evil, even if we undergo countless sufferings."[2]

Thomas à Kempis raises the question: "Do you know of any saint who, during his or her life, was without the cross and some affliction?" He answers in the negative and notes that just as Christ suffered so will we. He calls this the "royal way," not the way of deprivation. And he goes on to note that spiritual maturity does not bring about less suffering, but more. He writes: "The higher we advance in spirit, the heavier will be the crosses that we bear, because the pain of exile from God increases in proportion to our love for God."[3]

From these and other forebears of the Christian faith, we note that living the Christian life includes ongoing participation in the difficulties of life. The Christian is "in Christ" and is sheltered in his love and care. But the Christian is also "in the world" and experiences both its resources and blessings, and its problems and crises.

This means that the Christian is "torn." He is blessed in Christ, but suffers life's difficulties. She has come home to the beauty of God as Father, Son, and Holy Spirit, but is still only a pilgrim who often has to travel life's difficult roads.

Theologically this is construed as living the "yet and not-yet" nature of the kingdom of God. Christians live between the times of the first and

1. Ringma and Alexander, eds., *Of Martyrs, Monks, and Mystics*, 77.

2. Ringma and Alexander, eds., *Of Martyrs, Monks, and Mystics*, 360.

3. Ringma and Alexander, eds., *Of Martyrs, Monks, and Mystics*, 133.

second coming of Christ. They are too late for the world's enchantment, but too early for the joys of heaven.

When Crises Come

Early Christianity grew in persecution and martyr blood. But health crises, natural disasters, and invasions also came their way. There was no such a thing as Christians being magically spared from life's calamities. And there was no such a thing as a common Christian response to crises. Some saw a crisis as the judgment of God on the world. Others saw it as the fires of purgation to cleanse the church. Others, again, saw natural disasters and pandemics as a sign of the soon return of Christ. And for yet others, it was an opportunity to care for the needy and to spread the good news of the gospel of Christ.

Pandemics occurred in the first centuries of the spread of Christianity. The Antonine Plague, possibly a strain of smallpox, lasted from c. 165 to 189 CE. The Plague of Cyprian, which caused haemorrhagic fevers resulting in up to 5,000 deaths per day, lasted from c. 249 to 262 CE. In these circumstances Christians, who were seen not to honor local deities, were often targeted as the sole cause of the pandemic.[4] However, Christians in return often blamed society for worshipping false gods and resisting the gospel. But many Christians were moved to provide practical help and care. The historian Geoffrey Blainey points out that while "the pagan religions rarely offered help" in times of crisis, "many Christians, especially women, were willing to nurse the sick and take food to their [neighbors'] homes."[5] Blainey comments: "Christians received much more praise than blame during epidemics, and they coped more easily with the trauma and dislocation of illness, and the approach of death."[6]

But there was much more that the early Christians had to contend with, including brutal suppression and persecution. The Roman Emperor Decius from 250 CE onward waged a decade-long "war" against Christians where "thousands . . . were mutilated, wounded or killed."[7]

4. Flexsenhar, "How Ancient Christians responded to pandemics."
5. Blainey, *A Short History of Christianity*, 68.
6. Blainey, *A Short History of Christianity*, 69.
7. Blainey, *A Short History of Christianity*, 70.

Several centuries later an even greater tragedy struck Christian communities during the collapse of the Roman Empire. The Huns, Vandals, and Goths laid countries, cities, state infrastructure, and cathedrals to waste.

Bishop Possidius in his *Life of Augustine* spells out something of this tragedy and its impact on this great church leader:

> These days, therefore, that he lived through and endured . . . were the most bitter and mournful of his old age. For he saw cities overthrown in destruction, and the resident citizens, together with buildings on their lands, partly annihilated by the enemy's slaughter, and others driven into flight and dispersed. He saw churches stripped of priests . . . and holy virgins and all the monastics scattered in every direction . . . He saw some succumb to torture, and others slain by the sword . . . [others] losing their innocence . . . and [others] the harsh and evil treatment of slaves. He saw . . . church buildings in many places consumed by fire, the regular services which were due to God cease.[8]

In the midst of great tragedy this broken saint prays that God may "free this city." But if not, that God will "make his servants brave for enduring his will." And that personally God "may take me from this world unto himself."[9] Augustine died soon after.

From these very brief historical snippets we gain a much more realistic picture of a part of the history of Christianity. And to a greater or lesser degree, Christians over the long centuries to the present have been called to live their love of God and neighbor in times of war, changing governments, famines, natural disasters, and the grinding realities of poverty, illness, racism, and a lack of justice.

Christians in Society: A Dual Citizenship

While there may be some Christians who think that they should have nothing to do with society, many believe that God calls them to be witnesses of the gospel and to work to make society a better and more just place.

More specifically this is spelled out in three-dimensional terms. There is the upward movement in the worship of God. There is the inward movement in terms of spiritual transformation. And there is the outward movement to challenge the status quo and to bring about healing and renewal.

8. Ringma and Alexander, eds., *Of Martyrs, Monks, and Mystics*, 41.
9. Ringma and Alexander, eds., *Of Martyrs, Monks, and Mystics*, 41.

The above means that Christians are called to build the faith community and to transform their world. The implication of this is that they participate in a dual citizenship. They are part of the "kingdom of heaven" through Christ. And they are citizens of their country and seek to contribute to the shalom in society.

Being part of both creates *tensions*. And in the history of the church these tensions have resulted in pendulum swings. Sometimes, Christians have sought to be too heavenly minded, but no earthly good. This means that they lived a world-denying form of Christianity. At other times, Christians have been so enamored with their culture and its norms and values, that they felt that they had nothing to contribute, and in that lost the power of the gospel and failed in the task of prophetic witness. In holding this view, they embraced an overly world-affirming form of Christianity. And there have been periods in the history of the church where the church sought to dominate and control society.[10]

While somewhat overdrawn, H. Richard Niebuhr has set out the above scenarios in his classic *Christ and Culture*. But Niebuhr also cites two other models. The one sees the church as the transformer of society. The other, sees the relationship between church and society in much more paradoxical or dialectic terms. The former sees the church playing an important role in shaping a society. But its weakness is that it assumes that only the church has good things to give and the society has nothing to offer. Clearly, this is an inadequate view. Society also contributes to human well-being. And there are times where society can provoke the church to greater fidelity as we have seen in the child abuse scandals, to name a current example.

To see church and society in a paradoxical or dialectic relationship is more to the point. Society can provide the context for human flourishing. And the church can play a healing and prophetic role where society fails in providing justice. Besides this, and most basically, the faith community provides inspiration and resources for spiritual wholeness through Christ's redemptive work and the ever-present healing and empowering spirit. And blessed in this way, the faith community can add goodness and beauty to our world.

In a nutshell, the point here is clear. Christians are in Christ and in the world. They are part of the church and members of society. They are called to love God and love the neighbor. They thus live the tension of a dual citizenship. To broadly restate a theme in the writings of Jacques

10. Niebuhr, *Christ and Culture*.

Ellul, in the Christian two worlds meet. On the one hand, there is the "stream" of the reign of God through the Spirit, and on the other, there is both the goodness and the idolatry of the world.[11] What this means is that the Christian is to be a person of discernment and is to act in the church and the world as one shaped by the gospel, seeking to follow in the way of Christ, inspired by the Spirit, and one who longs to see God's final future break into our lives and world. And in the grace of God, the Christian is to resist the idolatries of our age.

Inspiration from Our Ancient Forebears

From the above we can see a number of things. Our Christian forebears did not live their faith in an ideal world, but in one of goodness and disasters. Thus, their life with God had to be outworked in the face of difficulties. And difficulties always provide both blockages and opportunities. Thus, there are the "why, O God?" questions, and the "what are the open doors?" and "what can we do to serve?" openings.

We have also noted that in the long journey of the church in history, different responses have been made in how to engage the world. What we will do now is to see what we can learn from our ancient forebears in responding well in times of crisis. In summary form, these are some of themes that I can see in their extensive writings.

Acknowledging our Fears and Anxieties

There is no virtue in putting up a brave front. Nor is denial going to help us. We need to tell God, ourselves, and others the things that trouble us. And we are seldom anxious only about ourselves. We are also concerned about family and friends, but also about the nation as a whole. St. Augustine in the midst of calamities is deeply concerned about his friends. He writes: "we are anxious that they might suffer from famine, war, disease, captivity . . . but we also painfully dread that their friendship may deteriorate into deceitfulness."[12]

11. Ellul, *The Presence of the Kingdom.*

12. Ringma and Alexander, eds., *Of Martyrs, Monks, and Mystics*, 306.

Embracing Loss

Times of crisis are times of loss. People lose their jobs and their health. They also lose their routines, sense of equilibrium, and emotional well-being. They may well lose more. And some may lose their faith because they are disappointed that God did not prevent the troubles that have come their way. St. Augustine notes that loss is a form of suffering that brings "pangs that tear the heart."[13] And St. Basil in describing his difficult circumstances speaks of being "bereft of the solace that I [once] possessed."[14] In embracing loss and acknowledging all that comes in loss's wake, there is the call to come with our emptiness to God and to seek God's protection. A prayer from the *Carmina Gadelica* reads: "I set the keeping of Christ about you, I set the guarding of God with you, To possess you, to protect you, From drowning, from danger, from loss."[15]

Identifying with the Suffering God

Pain and loss can lead us to self-pity and despair. It can also lead us to a new identification. And for the Christian this can lead to a deeper relationship with God. Our suffering can make us more aware of the suffering of others, but also of the Suffering God. The thirteenth century Beguine, Hadewijch, notes that people want "to live with God in consolations and repose," but we should also be willing "to carry his [Christ's] cross with him, or want to hang on the cross with him."[16] Hadewijch continues that we are so oriented to gaining advantages for ourselves, and so many of us seek "our own interests." But we are called to "forsake all as Christ did."[17]

Wrestling in Prayer

When our normal way of life disintegrates, we are thrown into a tailspin. And in this place of uncertainty and vulnerability, the invitation to pray becomes all the more pressing. St. Augustine notes at this point we are much

13. Ringma and Alexander, eds., *Of Martyrs, Monks, and Mystics*, 306.
14. Ringma and Alexander, eds., *Of Martyrs, Monks, and Mystics*, 138.
15. Ringma and Alexander, eds., *Of Martyrs, Monks, and Mystics*, 239.
16. Ringma and Alexander, eds., *Of Martyrs, Monks, and Mystics*, 182.
17. Ringma and Alexander, eds., *Of Martyrs, Monks, and Mystics*, 182.

more likely to see our true status: "we are all beggars before God."[18] John Cassian, the monastic formator, highlights that different circumstances call forth different types of prayer. He notes: "We pray one way when we are invigorated by spiritual achievements, and another way when we are cast down by the burden of attacks."[19] And thus in times of crisis, we may cry out to God, lament, and express our fears and anger. But we are invited to persevere. Better our cries to God than our sullen silence. The unknown author of the spiritual classic *The Book of Privy Counselling* reminds us: "So persevere in prayer with humility and great desire, for it is a work that begins on earth, but will go on without end into eternity."[20]

Practical Help

Times of crisis and difficulty can call forth the worst and the best in us. The worst, by way of example, is when people hoard food while others starve, and steal when homes have been abandoned due to floods. But the opposite is also true. People reach out to help each other, particularly those who are most vulnerable. St. Maximus the Confessor points out that "we shall be judged for the evil we have done, but especially for the good we have neglected, and for the fact that we have not loved the neighbor."[21] St. Augustine makes the point that at all times one should not be so caught up with contemplation so as "not to think of his [her] neighbor's welfare." On the other hand, one should not be so busy so as "not to seek after contemplation."[22]

The Quest for Justice

Times of crisis impact the poor and vulnerable disproportionally. Therefore, a pandemic, war, or major natural disaster highlights the plight of the poor, who often fall off our radar screen. In response, we are called to practical help that may be as basic as food and shelter. But we are also called to engage in the far more difficult and long-term quest for justice. The church

18. Ringma and Alexander, eds., *Of Martyrs, Monks, and Mystics*, 334.
19. Ringma and Alexander, eds., *Of Martyrs, Monks, and Mystics*, 33.
20. Ringma and Alexander, eds., *Of Martyrs, Monks, and Mystics*, 319.
21. Ringma, *Hear the Ancient Wisdom*, 101.
22. Butler, *Western Mysticism*, 165.

father Methodius, in his *Oration on the Psalms,* cries out: "Blessed is he who comes in the name of the Lord: the one for the many; to deliver the poor out of the hands of those who oppress them . . . from those who bring the poor to spoil."[23] St. Irenaeus calls all to "rendering to the lowly what is right and equitable and fair." This, he says, "corresponds to the exaltation and sublimity of God's justice."[24] And finally, St. John Chrysostom calls Christians to an orthopraxis. He exclaims: but those possessing much should "sell fields, sell houses, and vessels of gold and silver, and give to the poor." He continues: "supply what is needed, heal the sick, free such as are in straits [difficulties], some . . . deliver from bonds . . . release those in mines . . . [and] those who are captives." He then asks the provocative question: whose side are you on? On the side of those "gathering gold," or on the side of those who are "doing away with calamities"?[25]

Entering More Deeply into the Mystery of God

When problems come, we want answers. These are seldom forthcoming. We can't readily explain why bad things happen, but that they do is a fact of life. St. John Chrysostom gives some practical pastoral advice: "Do not enquire too curiously concerning his [God's] treatment, nor demand an account of it from him."[26] Hilary of Poitiers reminds us that "his [God's] greatness is too vast for our comprehension" and adds "but not for our faith."[27] But it may well be that even our faith stumbles. And better a faith that is tried in the "fires" of life's challenges than a faith that is only sculpted in the places of security and safety. Finally, Meister Eckhart makes the point that not only is God shrouded in mystery, but even God's word remains hidden in so many ways. He continues: "because it is hidden, one must always pursue it."[28]

23. Ringma and Alexander, eds., *Of Martyrs, Monks, and Mystics*, 366.
24. Ringma and Alexander, eds., *Of Martyrs, Monks, and Mystics*, 305.
25. Ringma and Alexander, eds., *Of Martyrs, Monks, and Mystics*, 190.
26. Ringma and Alexander, eds., *Of Martyrs, Monks, and Mystics*, 204.
27. Ringma and Alexander, eds., *Of Martyrs, Monks, and Mystics*, 391.
28. Ringma and Alexander, eds., *Of Martyrs, Monks, and Mystics*, 385.

Conclusion

In this reflection, we have noted that crises and difficulties are a part of life and that our Christian forebears were all too aware of life's precariousness. They, like us, lived their faith in a beautiful yet broken world; in times of peace and of war; in times of plenty and in hunger. And they knew the realities of epidemics and of nature's fury.

While there were times when the faith community did not respond well to crises and people in need, the overwhelming witness is that Christians sought to serve others in times of darkness and difficulty. And in brief form, I have sought to spell out what the more typical responses of our ancient forebears have been in times of need.

In our present challenging times, we too need to make our responses. And it is the intention of this reflection that we may be encouraged and find inspiration from our ancient Christians forebears. While we may wish that we could do a lot, we often have to do the little. Meister Eckhart reminds us: "Now some people despise the little things of life." He continues: "It is their mistake, for they thus prevent themselves from getting God's greatness out of these little things."[29]

A present-day example of responding to the needs of others while severely impacted themselves comes from our colleagues from Asian Theological Seminary in Manila, Philippines. While seriously affected by COVID-19 themselves and without sufficient funds for faculty and staff salaries, they embarked on helping two poor communities and the nearby overcrowded prison with much needed food and infection prevention provisions. They demonstrated love of neighbor in a time of crisis and embodied the practical wisdom and compassion of our ancient forebears. We too are called to demonstrate kindhearted generosity to others in this time of need.

29. Ringma and Alexander, eds., *Of Martyrs, Monks, and Mystics*, 114.

Store up for yourselves treasures in heaven,

where neither moth nor rust consumes

and where thieves do not break in and steal.

For where your treasure is, there your heart will be also
(Matt 6:20–21 NRSV).

Lord, we speak out our trust that you care for us even in times of economic crisis.

We choose to focus on your kingdom,

rather than on our own safety and security.

We ask you to make us more like you, generous to all.

Help us to live as stewards of your earth, caring for your world and those within it.

9

Treasure in Heaven: Economy and the Kingdom

Terry Gatfield

The present economic crisis has come as a shock to the majority of Western nations, where there has been a long honeymoon offering peace, security, and prosperity. Australia, from the vantage point of my desk, has enjoyed twenty-six years of continuous economic growth.[1] It came through the Global Financial Crisis (GFC) relatively unscathed, it has restructured its economy and export markets, and the country has not had to face any major crisis. The tide has now turned, and for the first time every sector of the economy is affected, including education, health, food production, logistics, policing, retailing and wholesaling, entertainment, the arts, public gatherings, religious assemblies, and governance. The list is endless. Changes mandated are not optional, and effect all in every domain of life. There are numerous articles written about COVID-19, but this chapter is about the economy. The questions that need to be raised are: firstly, *is this going to be a financial Armageddon?* and secondly, *for the Christian, what light and hope is found in the Scriptures to aid our understanding?*

The news most of us hear is about the spread of the pandemic along with the immediate impact on the economy and the calls for growth, jobs, and government payouts, with little explanation of the big picture of how the economy functions. Perhaps that is just as well as, in general, an

1. *Foreign Policy*, "Australia."

understanding of economics, its language, the cultural context, and its personalities are often out of reach of the average person. Perhaps for most of us the subject of economics produces yawn-inducing slumber—no wonder it is often called "the dismal science."[2]

In order to get a firmer understanding of economics, I went to see my friend Benson, who has a post-graduate degree in economics. He has also spent time in scouring the political, national, and international horizons, as well as the social and Christian frameworks, in some depth. However, what I thought were two relatively simple questions turned out to be no small task. There was some groundwork I had to come to terms with before Benson responded to my queries. I have recorded the essence of our conversation.

"Benson, thanks for taking the time to respond to the questions about economics and the COVID-19 crisis. What is your thinking?"

"Well, that depends on your understanding—and what's on your mind's horizon regarding economics. Please share your thoughts."

I had forgotten that Benson would often respond to a question with another question! "Well, I believe it is about money, taxation, government spending, balance of payments, and such things," I responded.

"Yes, it can be, but it is better to think about it from a far wider perspective. The word economics, *oiko-nomia*, comes from ancient Greece, via Aristotle. The two words, *oiko-nomia*, taken together refer to the science of household management or household administration. The idea of economics is that it is a function inherent in every individual, family, institution, and form of governance. Economics is the air we breathe every day and is not simply about money but resources. This is important! Resources embrace materials, time, and humanity—finite and infinite. Money is simply a common measure. The word *economics* is mainly used in the broad context that focuses on production, consumption, and distribution of goods and services, or, another way to express it, who gets what, how, and when. It is also about redistribution of wealth to assist in building an equitable society. For example, people who earn a higher income pay more income tax and some of that tax goes to support those on pensions as well as welfare recipients. Of course, in the current crisis, there are special payments taken from government revenues to assist a wider band of people in need. Economics affects the life and domain of every person, not just government policy-makers."

2. Carlyle, "Occasional Discourse on the Negro Question," 672.

"You said it is a science though it doesn't sound much like a science; seems more like a knee jerk action on the run," I said.

"Yes, it is often termed a science, but we should not get too carried away by that idea, as it is not a true science. A true science is something that is universally accepted under specified conditions that have been validated by observation and experimentation, and can be replicated at any time. Examples of a true science are legion, such as two atoms of hydrogen link with one atom of oxygen to produce water, which has defined boiling and freezing points at specific pressures. Another could be the speed of light or the gravitational pull of the earth. Sometimes the laws are called Newtonian, after Isaac Newton, when things can be measured in an absolute sense and their relationship with other matter can be predetermined. Economics, unlike true sciences, where outcomes can be determined with certainty, is more like a bundle of principles linked in a unique way to complex and particular situations, and to all manner of human systems. Economics is a pragmatic collection of ideals socially determined and influenced by a myriad of factors, such as the influence of certain individuals, institutional forms, educational understandings, conflict engagements and outcomes, historical events, various philosophical ideals and notions, and all manner of religious beliefs. *Economic thoughts and determinations are a messy basket of factors*. There is never one economic ideal or policy that fits all situations. Economics, and economic policies and understandings, are not stable or rigid and their outcomes are organic. They are like shifting sands, some are good and appropriate others may be disastrous. And they change markedly overtime. Do not look for everyone to be on the same page—agreements in the social malaise of economics are quite rare. There is an old saying, 'If all the economists were joined head to toe in a straight line, they would never reach a conclusion.'"

Oh my, I was starting to feel a little uncomfortable, realizing I was seeking the comfort of certainty, a certainty I could trust and have some faith in. I paused, waiting for Benson to deliver. He didn't. I was the first to break the silence: "Surely the Bible is able to provide much wisdom for the Christian thinker to discern what is the correct understanding of economics?"

"So, you want me to address the second question first? A great idea. Always try to get your theological perspectives right and then examine your life and the culture you are immersed in. I like the imperative given by the Apostle Paul:

> So here's what I want you to do, God helping you: Take your everyday, ordinary life—your sleeping, eating, going-to-work, and walking-around life—and place it before God as an offering. Embracing what God does for you is the best thing you can do for him. Don't become so well-adjusted to your culture that you fit into it without even thinking. Instead, fix your attention on God. You'll be changed from the inside out. Readily recognize what he wants from you, and quickly respond to it. Unlike the culture around you, always dragging you down to its level of immaturity, God brings the best out of you, develops well-formed maturity in you." (Rom 12:12—all biblical references in this chapter are from *The Message*)

"Take heart and remember the phrase I just gave you, 'Always try to get your theological perspectives right and then examine your life, your relationships and the culture you are immersed in.' This is not always so easy, and it will be an ongoing process of continuing in participation with the Holy Spirit and spirit of Christ himself, through the Scriptures and his body—that is, the church. Take to heart the words mentioned, 'don't become so well-adjusted to your culture that you fit into . . . fix your attention on God.' This calls for discernment—deep discernment. And might I add, discernment not just from our own individualistic mind, but the shared mind of Christ in the community of faith. This is no easy task and bravery, transparency, honesty, humility, love, and compassion must rule your decision-making process. Don't let popular culture rule and dictate to your heart and mind, shaping your behavior in all things. Some things in our culture are to be commended, others perhaps, not so, and in those areas, we must be prepared to be countercultural."

"Benson, I have done a little homework on the subject of economics and the Bible and, although I cannot say it has been extensive, the journey has not been very helpful to date. Perhaps that is why I have come to you for some enlightenment and clarity."

"Let me guess a little about your search. You may have heard a lot about personal prosperity. That is, if I honor God in my right living, especially with my money, and in particular, through my tithing, offerings, and giving, I will be rewarded by God through increased prosperity. I would not be surprised if you uncovered much from the commentaries about national or global prosperity. Regarding economics and the individual, I expect you have found the ideas dressed up as immutable laws of the kingdom encapsulating verses such these from Genesis, Malachi, Luke, Matthew, and John:

> He created them male and female. God blessed them: Prosper! Reproduce! Fill Earth! Take charge! (Gen 1:28).
>
> Bring your full tithe to the Temple treasury so there will be ample provisions in my Temple. Test me in this and see if I don't open up heaven itself to you and pour out blessings beyond your wildest dreams (Mal 3:10).
>
> Give away your life; you'll find life given back, but not merely given back—given back with bonus and blessing. Giving, not getting, is the way. Generosity begets generosity (Luke 6:38).
>
> And then there's the story of the talents, telling how the master went off on a trip leaving three servants with five thousand dollars, two thousand, and one thousand respectively. The two with the higher amounts doubled the investment while the third, buried his saying it was the safer thing to do. The master was furious with this last servant saying he should have at least put it in the bank where it would have made some interest (Matt 25:14–27).
>
> I pray for good fortune in everything you do, and for your good health—that your everyday affairs prosper, as well as your soul! (3 John 2).

"Well that is a nice tight summary," I replied. "And yes, the verses most talked about did relate to individual prosperity. But this is the word of God, it is sacred text. Isn't there a Scripture that says something like 'all scripture is inspired by God?'"

"Yes, but as readers of the word we need a rich understanding of our cultural context and need to seek much wisdom and discernment in translating the Hebrew and Greek languages into English—it is no simple task. Some words are extremely difficult to get a one-to-one translation. There is a French phrase, *Traduire, c'est trahire*, which means 'to translate is to betray,' or 'all translation is treason.'[3] We need always to be in that space of continually suspending judgment in our translations. We are thrown so often by our Western cultural understanding and sometimes in the wrong direction. Our Bible translators in the vast majority of cases are males, born and bred in cultures where property, acquisition, and personal ownership are the norm, and these are supported by a legal and judicial system that largely favors the individual and their personal rights. We must have sensitivity in our translations as we cross the millennia of

3. Gorman, *Participating in Christ*, 118.

time, as well as engaging the complex cultural boundaries. On a more direct note it is essential in our reflections to be wholistic and avoid the errors of snatching odd verses, often out of context, just to support our own personal position of comfort derived from our own particular norms and preferences. A final note on this, but surely not just the last word: we in the West seem to be largely locked into a transactional relationship in our daily lives—that is: 'if I do that, then I expect you will do this!' So often we treat the Trinity like that with so little room for grace, mercy, and the sovereignty of God. Remember what Paul says: 'Fix your attention on God. You'll be changed from the inside out.'"

I felt a little overcome and somewhat bewildered as I expected Benson would give me a nice distilled package in response to my question about a biblical understanding of economics. My mind was set on discovering the right formula. Perhaps my disappointment was showing. Benson, an excellent reader of body language and the importance of silence, let me stew for some moments.

Finally, he continued, "I am not letting you off the hook lightly. This is hard work and the Scriptures should not be just a voice to support and endorse Western democracy, capitalism, private ownership, and individual rights. Scripture makes a careful response to all monarchical adoptions, tribal collective understandings, mercantilism, communism, fascism, socialism, feudalism, and any other 'ism' you want to mention. A great exponent of this thought is the French sociologist and lay theologian, Jacques Ellul. He, and many others, challenge the notion of a rigid and dogmatic Christian view of economics.[4] However, we should and must obtain certain God-given principles to guide us on our pilgrimage. Here are a few:

> *This is God's world and we are only tenants and temporary custodians;*
>
> *We are to be committed to be honest and caring stewards of all of God's creation;*
>
> *Resources and money are for the benefit and flourishing of all, not just ourselves and our own set of national interests;*
>
> *Take seriously the parable of the Talents;*
>
> *The love of money and the passion to obtain it, is the root of all evil;*
>
> *Store up treasure in heaven, not on earth;*

4. Ellul, *What I Believe*.

Follow the example of Christ, who came not to be served but to serve.

Benson continued: "We must echo the life, beauty, and wonder of the Trinity in our lives and in the use of resources for the benefit of the whole of creation, and not for our own selfish gains. We may not be able to have a nice concrete doctrine derived from the Scriptures, yet we do receive considerable insights from them to guide us. In addition, the Holy Spirit, prayer, wisdom from the body of Christ, meditation, and contemplation can help us. But, most important for us as followers of Christ is to gain a renewed heart and mind. Our dependency should be focused on God and his kingdom, and less and less on ourselves. That's what it means to have treasure in heaven."

Again, there was a long silence from me as I tried to let some of Benson's wisdom penetrate the fundamentalist position that had been my comfort, security, and friend for many years. Slowly my brain engaged with my vocal cords. "I like what you have said, Benson, but I need to let so much of what you have said, sit with me."

"Take time my friend, you may need to give what I said lots of space. In the meantime, let's see if I can address your other question, '*Is COVID-19 going to be a financial Armageddon?*' I am not a prophet, and I do not want to be definitive as my time of speaking with you is in COVID-19's early days and, in the main, my understanding is somewhat limited to its effects in Australia. It may help you to see my optimistic attitude by looking at how advanced, but by no means perfect, our contemporary life is. Our present Western systems are a hybrid of policies and actions developed over centuries, perhaps millennia. Rather than exploring this complex history, let us consider two basic positions—the two extremes. First, the command economy. In this, the State fully owns the means of production and delivery of services, and the State is responsible for their distribution. Examples were the old Soviet ideals of the early 1900s. The process was a mega-failure and is largely defunct. The only remaining economy still running along those lines is North Korea. The other extreme is where production of goods and services is determined by market supply and demand with no government market interference. Price determines who gets what and when. The government is only there to foster trade and to assist in the development of the economy. This was the dream of the so-called Mercantilists of the 1800s. Every country is a bit of a hybrid of these two extremes. Hence, we call it a mixed economy. In every country and economy, governments place restrictions and controls on the market in so many ways. Examples are legion and include issues related to personal safety, drug and alcohol consumption, pollution, gun sales, disposal of waste, trading hours, working conditions, labeling and consumer information on food stuffs, and, for many countries, a fair wage policy—it is a very long list. However, governments assist and promote trade in a variety of ways, such as building roads, rail and air transport infrastructure, providing research, develop grants, assisting in trade missions, and providing aid to the rural sector when necessary, as well as assisting the unemployed in times of need and seasonal adjustment."

I responded, "Yes, I can see that a little more clearly, but what is the correct blend? How far should the free market go and how much should the government intervene by helping or hindering?"

"That is the million-dollar question, and there is no simple answer. It is like shifting sands. One day the sands are here and the next there. Constant adjustments are needed to find an optimal position—not a maximized one. The free market is a wonderful thing as through the price mechanism consumers can determine what will be purchased and therefore what will be produced. The so-called founder of contemporary economics, Adam Smith, in 1759, called it the 'invisible hand.' Please don't think this was a religious understanding involving God. It is a simple statement how, in a collective sense, markets are shaped and formed in a way not clearly seen. You should consider that, in the main, markets are a very efficient and an economical means of getting the right goods to consumers. But markets are subject to what we call 'failure.'"

I asked, "Do you mean that markets collapse through things like cheats, scammers, and fraudsters or does it relate to the Great Depression and the GFC of some years ago?"

"None of these. It is technical term used by economists to say that not everything produced and consumed would be best served by the free market through the price mechanism. They refer to things like health, education, law enforcement, the arts, museums, roads as well as street lighting, and footpaths. These are for everybody, not just those who could afford them. They are there for the 'common good.' Sometimes there is a market mix, such as between private and public hospitals. Some countries lean towards privatization of everything, trying to make most social services marketable as free market commodities. But it is questionable whether or not the outcomes are good for the nation as a whole. There are numerous examples where privatization has not produced the economic or the ideal social outcomes. An example can be found in America. Health care in the USA, which is in the main privatized, absorbs 18 percent of their GDP, and it is estimated that it will be 32 percent by the year 2030.[5] In Australia, where health care is substantively public, the costs are attributed to only 10 percent of GDP.[6] Australia is fortunate that in the current time of the COVID-19 crisis there has been the safety net of publicly funded health facilities available to everyone, not just the ones who can work the financial markets to their advantage.

"I hope that clears the air a little about market failure. And remember, privatization of public goods is a relatively new phenomena in economic thought and had been accelerated by certain individuals in the Western world through the likes of Thatcher, Reagan, and our own John Howard in Australia. Consideration should be given to whether this is a good ethical position to be taking, especially for the Christian. The jury has been out for some, but apathy seems to rule the day for most people."

I was getting a little disturbed about the facts which were being outlined, and I wanted more direction about the current crises as it seemed to be not only about readjusting, but looking to the future with a high degree of uncertainty. Selfishly, my mind was a little locked into my own country. It seems that the nation has almost come to a standstill with a very mediocre workforce to fill the national coffers. My mind was filled with thoughts that the treasury was a little pot of gold and now it was being milked by the needs of individuals who could not work, and by those dependent on welfare and who would require ongoing financial support. This problem appeared to be multiplied by the fact that recipients were no longer taxpayers and direct contributors to the process. I think Benson was a mind-reader as he quickly addressed those issues that would aid my understanding.

"It may be wise to introduce to you a concept that may give you a little hope in this time of crisis—the multiplier effect—a darling principle in economics. This refers to one dollar earned generating many more dollars for the community. This is how it works. Let's suppose I am a farmer growing apples to sell in the market. For every dollar of apples sold some of that money will go to the suppliers of fertilizers, boxes, transport, etc. All of the participants will then have money to spend on vehicles, food, housing, insurance; the money going around in a large circle that financially benefits others. In effect, it multiplies itself on its journey. One dollar

5. Mikulic, "U.S. national health expenditure as percent of GDP from 1960 to 2020."

6. Hinton, "Health expenditure as percentage of the gross domestic product (GDP) in Australia from 2006 to 2017."

becomes many. Yet, it cannot go on forever as there are leakages, and one of the major leakage points is the propensity of individuals to save. If people save a proportion of their money it becomes frozen; the bigger the saving the less the multiplier. Less money then goes around to others."

I was pondering on how that seemed counter-intuitive to my natural thinking. My reaction in times of crisis is to get a little more conservative and frugal, and put even more money aside—you know, money for a rainy day. I voiced my understanding to Benson.

He replied, "Look, my friend, if everybody saved all they earned, hypothetically of course, as that would be impossible, the world's economic framework would totally collapse. Spending in a time of crisis is essential. Here is an example: for every dollar earned ten cents gets saved so that ninety cents are passed on to others to spend. They then pass on their share of the ninety cents less their saving portion of ten cents. In this situation the multiplier would be a factor of ten. One extra dollar for an individual becomes ten dollars through the community. However, if fifty cents were saved then the multiplier becomes two, meaning only two dollars get passed down through the community. If the whole dollar was saved, then nothing gets passed down. There are a number of leakages, but one of the main ones is the issue of savings. The more people save the smaller the multiplier."

"Isn't it strange?" I responded. "I have always thought savings to be a great idea."

Benson was quick to reply: "Yes, it is, but savings at times of an economic crisis does not work in the aggregate—in fact, it may hinder the economy. What is needed is often an economic stimulus. A direct injection of money into the economy by the government that boosts household spending and captures the multiplier effect. Remember, one dollar will become much more than that dollar. It usually works, but there is no guarantee. A good example is Japan, where the government has been overactive in giving stimulus after stimulus to little or no effect. Japanese consumers do not have a culture of spending like we do—thrift is more important to them. Perhaps one of the best examples of a direct injection of money into the economy, which we now call a stimulus, arrived during the Great Depression of the 1930s. It was global and, over about a decade, suffering was immense with unemployment topping 25 percent combined with little or no social security measures that are now common to us. I won't go into the reasons as that will take time, but what I can say is that the main reason why the Depression lifted was due to government intervention—by starting substantial public works programs and thereby reducing unemployment, which encouraged spending. Through the multiplier effect the economy began buzzing again. One of the principle architects was John Maynard Keynes. He was an Oxford economist who was highly published, extremely controversial, and largely opposed to the economic traditions of that time. His thoughts were largely rejected by the English conservative neo-classical schools. The Americans, who suffered a huge depression crisis, through Keynes's economic and social insights, were able to lift the country out of darkness and poverty. Two of Keynes's principal ideas were to get the government to engage in capital work programs and reduce taxation. The effect was to kick-start the economy. The momentum carried the economy in a forward direction into growth, moving it towards full employment and substantially reducing the effects of poverty. For this we must thank Keynes. Most other Western countries eventually followed the USA during that time."

I finally blurted: "I think this is interesting, but I am not certain about its relevance. Where are you going with this, and how does this relate to the current crisis that we are facing?"

"Well, it's the issue of government-induced stimulus through engaging in supporting employment in industries that are forced to close their doors on a temporary basis and to offer additional hardship payments in other areas. This is what we call Keynesian. It runs counter to what we term the neo-classical principles of the free markets where there is little or no direct government intervention. More recently, we dipped into the Keynesian principle in Australia in 2008 in the days of the GFC. Then Prime Minister Rudd put $22.5 billion into the economy to prevent an economic recession.[7] It worked and there is hope that the Keynesian ideals will save us from digging a big and deeper hole in our present economy. It is interesting that virtually every advanced nation in the world is living in a Keynesian twilight."

My further question came from a deep concern: "But Benson, where does the money come from? We don't have geese to lay golden eggs!"

"That is true. The money has to be raised. This is done by borrowing, mainly through government issued bonds. These are sold nationally and on the global market at a certain percentage interest rate. After many years, the bonds are redeemed when the economy may be in better shape to make the payment; alternatively, new bonds can be printed. It may increase our indebtedness, but if the value of the debt is smaller than the

7. Robinson, "Rudd's Stimulus Package."

increased benefit, we are in front. Don't we do this when we personally consider buying a house or any another kind of asset like a car or education? But don't be overly concerned by our national debt. Australia is not a highly indebted nation and our economic security is very strong. The best measure is to look at the ratio of total country debt to that of total GDP. Much worse is Japan at 237 percent.[8] That means that if all the total income of individuals in Japan was used to pay back what is owing, and nothing else, it would take 2.37 years! The USA is estimated at 136 percent,[9] while Australia is a mere 41 percent.[10] Our borrowings are low by world standards. Australia, then, is a very safe and economically stable country, relatively speaking. Safe and assured for bond buyers."

I responded, "But what about money supply: won't that dry up if there are insufficient taxpayers to keep the system going?"

"Well, some of that will come from bonds, as I mentioned, but it will also be supplied by printing more money. This is a newly emerging school of thought which is gaining credibility and is called the Modern Monetary Theory (MMT). As Australia has a floating currency, like the USA, England, and a few others, it is not linked to a gold standard or to any other currency. This means that we can print as much money as we like. It is a quasi-Keynesian approach. The major caveats are inflation and foreign exchanges. MMT thought is starting to take hold in Treasury circles as it could prove a useful tool to assist in keeping our economy in momentum. Though in early days, we can be relatively assured and relaxed that our economy can survive even in dark and difficult times."

I finally responded: "Benson, this has been an interesting journey and at times you have touched, by inference, aspects related to ethics which impacts on Christian thought regarding money and the economy. I like the way you have given a little insight into how the economy is readjusting nationally and globally to the current epidemic. It gives me a little more hope for a brighter future."

Benson and I parted company. I had hoped that he would be able to provide me with a nice basket of certainties about economics. That did not materialize, but he did give me a better foundation in finding greater hope and meaning. I increasingly find myself without the power or skill to affect

8. *Trading Economics*, "Japan General Government Gross Debt to GDP."

9. Amadeo, "US National Debt by Year Compared to GDP and Major Events."

10. Australian Government Data, "Australian National Debt Explained—With Real Time Debt Clock."

any outcomes—save in the mercy of God. I am now more trusting that his sovereign will shall infuse our governments, institutions, and churches in keeping our world flourishing till his return . . . and that his will shall be done on earth as it is in heaven.

I will continue the pilgrimage, even in time of great global distress and economic concerns.

For nation will rise against nation, and kingdom against kingdom;

there will be earthquakes in various places;

there will be famines . . . (Mark 13:8)

Lord, In our mourning, grieving, and lament,

we engage with you in the context of the pain and suffering, which is all around us.

You do not require that we gloss over the grave reality of the situation,

but rather validate our feelings of despair, grief, lostness,

and even anger that a crisis engenders.

You do not turn away as our laments break out in protest against injustice and boldly call on you to act.

It is in your attentiveness to the deep cries of our hearts

that we can imagine with confidence a new future

that comes out of an enlarged understanding of who you are,

and what you can do in a seemingly hopeless situation.

10

When Disaster Strikes

Lament, Liminality, and Living in the In-Between

Athena E. Gorospe

There is no doubt that the COVID-19 pandemic is a disaster on a global and massive scale. And because it affects both wealthy and poorer nations, both the privileged and the disadvantaged, one cannot marshal the resources of one country or sector of society to help another, although undoubtedly, the greatest impact would be on the poor and the marginalized. Similar to all disaster situations, whether natural or human, people are robbed of the security of their daily routines and social interactions, and are placed in vulnerable positions.

The worst thing we can do is to act as if things are normal. Indeed, often the first instinct is to try to take charge of the situation so that we can assure ourselves that things are not spiraling out of control. The problem, however, is that we fall back into old ways of operating, which may no longer work in the new setting. Moreover, the reality is, we are not in control—the virus is continuing to wreak havoc even in communities that earlier thought they had the virus under control.

We are all aware of the economic repercussions of a prolonged lockdown, especially in vulnerable communities. In the Philippines where

I live, we have jeepney[1] drivers begging for food on the streets; elderly people breaking out in tears because they were not given the promised financial help; locally stranded individuals who have lost their jobs in Metro Manila, camping out on the dirt road, waiting for a ride back to their provinces; and overseas Filipino workers losing their jobs, getting sick, and then dying and being buried in a foreign land, separated from their families, who could not even get a glimpse of their bodies or visit their burial place. Then, there is the worsening mental health situation, regardless of what nation a person belongs to, leading to depression, self-harm, and explosions of anger and violence.

What is sad is that governments can capitalize on these vulnerabilities—consolidating their own power and becoming more repressive in the process. For example, during the past four months of lockdown, the Philippine government has passed an anti-terror law that is similar to the Hong Kong Security Law.[2] It successfully shut down a major television network and convicted the editor and reporter of an online newspaper that criticizes the government. And now it is threatening to take over the management of telephone companies that run the country's internet network, regulate social media to stifle dissent, and make moves to change the Constitution to extend the term limits of current political officials.

However, an opposite mind-set may also develop. Instead of denying reality and acting as if things are the same as before, we may become completely immobilized by fear and a sense of powerlessness, so that we do not act at all even in the face of great need. Worse, we can retreat into an unreal spiritualized world, mouthing vain platitudes of God's triumph, sovereignty, and control, which have little or no connection with the reality around us. We saw this incongruity in the aftermath of Typhoon Haiyan (Yolanda) in 2013.[3] Several teams from my seminary went to the disaster

1. A jeepney is one of the main public transportation in the Philippines. It is modeled after the US military jeeps used in World War II but has an extended back that can seat up to sixteen people.

2. Some of the provisions of the Philippine Anti-Terror law include: expanding the definition of terrorism to include anything that "creates a serious risk to public safety," which can be interpreted broadly; warrantless arrest up to fourteen days that may be extended up to twenty-one days; determining who is a terrorist or a terrorist group is left to the Anti-Terrorism Council, consisting of officials from the Executive Branch; and provides no compensation for those who were mistakenly arrested. See *Official Gazette*, "The Anti-Terrorism Act of 2020."

3. Asian Theological Seminary, "ATS Teams Go to Disaster Areas."

areas to facilitate psycho-spiritual processing to affected communities[4] and, while doing so, attended worship services in various churches. It was incongruous hearing the worship teams singing triumphalistic songs amidst the ruins of church buildings, with the majority of the members having no roofs over their heads or food to eat, and people wandering around the streets, looking shell-shocked. Pastors, on the other hand, had nothing much to say, except to assert that God is in control. It felt a bit surreal.

The question, however, is: How do we navigate a response between over-control and paralysis?

Lament and the Expressions of Grief and Protest

The psalms of lament provide some insight for us. "Lament in the Bible is a liturgical response to the reality of suffering and engages God in the context of pain and trouble."[5] Thus, these psalms do not gloss over the grave reality of the situation, but validate the feelings of despair, grief, lostness, and even anger that a crisis engenders.[6] At the same time, they break out in protest against injustice and boldly call on God to act,[7] imagining with confidence a new future that comes out of an enlarged understanding of who God is and what God can do in a seemingly hopeless situation.

These twin actions—grief and protest—accompanied by bold prayer and courageous hope, which are all captured by the form of a lament, are important elements that can possibly point the way ahead for us. In grief, we honestly cry out to God the pain and anguish of the situation. In protest, we ask why? and how long?, refusing to accept a situation of injustice, dysfunctional systems, and unbridled use of power by those who exploit the vulnerabilities of the situation for their own ends.

Most psalms of lament end with expressions of confidence that God will intervene, that the distress will end, that the sufferer will be vindicated and judgment will be meted out to the oppressors and mockers of God's justice. Nevertheless, there are some psalms that lack resolution,

4. Psycho-spiritual support is psychological first aid given to vulnerable communities but which "integrates psychological tools and spiritual/theological resources and employs culturally and spiritually sensitive processes." See Manzanilla-Manalo, "Psycho-Spiritual Support in the Aftermath of Supertyphoon Yolanda/Haiyan."

5. Rah, *Prophetic Lament*, 21.

6. Brueggemann, "From Hurt to Joy, From Death to Life," 4.

7. Williams, "Biblical Lament and Political Protest."

where the movement juxtaposes lament and praise, alternates them, or ends in lament rather than in praise.[8]

Moreover, the lament form in itself is inadequate to capture the process that is necessary to transition to a future with new possibilities. It is actually the movement in the different types of psalms, as they are taken together, that can act as a resource to portray the shift from the old to the new. Walter Bruggemann refers to this movement as one of orientation, disorientation, and reorientation.[9]

The psalms of praise—focusing on who God is—express the *orientation* phase, which affirms life's certainties in God's sovereignty, faithfulness, and love. However, intense suffering and injustice challenge these certainties. Suddenly, the old formulas no longer work as one grapples with the unknown, and one's belief in the goodness of God is put in doubt as questions are left unanswered. This is the *disorientation* phase, which is expressed in the psalms of lament, in which questions and grievances—even if they are directed towards God—are given space to be uttered in God's presence.

This honesty is needed to move to the next phase. In *reorientation*, our faith is affirmed, but it is a faith that has gone through the fire. This is expressed in the psalms of thanksgiving, which tell the story of distress and salvation, then end with a declaration of God's goodness, power, and love. Nevertheless, the affirmations are not the same as before. We say "God is good" but this is no longer a trite phrase because it contains all the pain and doubts that one has gone through, and thus expresses a deeper understanding of who God is.

This movement of back and forth, however, is a spiral rather than linear.[10] It is not the case that after we reach the point of reorientation that we no longer go back to disorientation. The new point can be challenged again by another crisis, so one enters into another threshold experience that leads to a fresh reorientation. But each cycle incorporates both the old and the new learnings, so it is not circular, but spiral. Moreover, there are some things that are not completely resolved, as in the case of psalms that end with lament, or when the tension between lament and praise are kept through their

8. Villanueva, *The Uncertainty of Hearing*, 29.

9. Brueggemann, "Psalms and the Life of Faith," 6–10. For the threefold movement as applied to the pandemic, see International Ministries, "A Reflection on Disorientating Events."

10. Goldingay, "The Dynamic Cycle of Praise and Prayer in the Psalms," 88.

juxtaposition or interchange.[11] This implies that the process towards the new is never neat. There would be times when we think that we are making good progress; there would be days as well when we feel we are stuck and in a rut, or may even sense that we are going a few steps backward. And sometimes, the disorientation phase may be longer and more complicated than we ever expected. We want to move to the "new normal," but it is not happening as quickly or as straightforwardly as we have hoped.

Liminality and a Death-Like Experience

In recent years, there has been a lot of discussion about what anthropologists call "liminality."[12] Liminality is the in-between place between what used to be and what is going to be. Liminal events—and a pandemic can be one of them—are times of uncertainties and destabilizations. But it is precisely because of this that they can help in the shift from the old to the new. During liminal periods, old patterns and structures no longer operate, making it possible for new configurations to emerge, and thus allowing for transformation to take place.[13] For example, Israel's journey from Egypt to Canaan has a liminal stage. Between the initial separation from Egypt as marked by the exodus and the crossing of the Red Sea, and the new life in Canaan whose entry is marked by the crossing of the Jordan, there is a long interim period of wandering in the wilderness.[14]

However, such transitions are only possible if, during the liminal period, there is a death-like experience, in which we go through the pain of loss of what used to be. Metaphors associated with liminality speak of death, dissolution, or decomposition[15] because through the act of separation from the old way of life, the liminal subject is symbolically undergoing death.[16] As Charles Ringma says in chapter 2, "Rather than seeing loss as an enemy,

11. Villanueva, *Uncertainty of Hearing*, 101–31, 133–62, 163–85.

12. Carson, *Liminal Reality and Transformational Power*; van Gennep, *The Rites of Passage*; Turner, *The Forest of Symbols* and *The Ritual Process*.

13. Turner, *Forest of Symbols*, 97, 102; Carson, *Liminal Reality*, 1–14.

14. Cohn, *The Shape of Sacred Space*, 7–23.

15. Turner, *Ritual Process*, 95. Other metaphors include being in darkness, or are connected to the wilderness, to the womb, to invisibility, or to an eclipse.

16. Turner, *Forest of Symbols*, 96. In Exodus 4, this death is evoked in Yahweh's threat to the life of Moses and his family.

we may learn to see it as friend. And loss is a companion to emptiness, and emptiness may be the seed-bed for a new receptivity."[17]

Biblical characters such as Jacob and Moses, who went through a liminal experience, experienced a death-like or threatening encounter. Nevertheless, after their harrowing experiences, both men experienced a change of status and relationship, marked in Jacob's case by the change of his name to Israel and reconciliation with his brother, and in the case of Moses by the rite of circumcision and incorporation back to his people, the Israelites.[18]

In Jacob's return to Canaan, after many years away from his homeland, he had a dangerous encounter with an unknown opponent, who struck him and made him limp, leaving an indelible mark throughout his life (Gen 32:22–32). This prepared him for his eventual reconciliation with his brother Esau, with Jacob approaching his brother with humility and generosity, in contrast to his previous action of stealing Esau's birthright and blessing (Gen 33:1–3, 5–11; cf. Gen 27:1–40). Esau, on the other hand, offered protection, which is a change from his previous stance of plotting murder against his brother (Gen 33:4, 12–15; cf. Gen 27:41–45).[19]

In the same way, Moses and his family's return to Egypt to take up his prophetic calling was mysteriously stopped by Yahweh, who threatened to kill him. Prior to this, Moses had an ambivalent identity—born a Hebrew, raised up an Egyptian, married to a Midianite wife and being content to live as a sojourner with the household of his Midianite father-in-law—and showing an indecisive and lukewarm response to God's call for him to lead the Israelites out of their oppression in Egypt to a new life in Canaan. The threat of death provided a way to resolve this ambivalence as Zipporah, despite her foreign ethnicity, makes the decisive move to circumcise their son, identifying the whole family as belonging unequivocally to Yahweh and to the people of Israel.[20]

The liminal period is uncomfortable and painful, but it is necessary. Hence, we should not rush quickly into the "new normal." We need time to process our longings in relation to the old life, especially the things we find difficult to relinquish and that we miss the most. This involves reflecting on

17. Ringma, chapter 2 of this book.

18. Römer, "De l'Archaïque au Subversif," 5; Robinson, "Zipporah to the Rescue," 451–52.

19. Molito, "God in the Face of the Other," 49–55.

20. Gorospe, *Narrative and Identity*, 191–97; 200–210 and "Old Testament Narratives in Context."

what we have lost and the many other forms of "dying" that we have experienced in the past months, during lockdown or otherwise. It means having the space and freedom to grieve the loss, alone or with others, and finding resources to cope with drastically changed circumstances. Hence, we must be willing to stay in the in-between, and seek to hear God better, and gain a new vision from a position of pain and loss. But how does one stay in the difficult place of uncertainty and loss without falling apart?

Living in the In-Between

Mark 13, the so-called "Little Apocalypse" because it has to do with the end times, can provide us with some insights regarding how to live life in the in-between. While the chapter touches on events leading to the end of human history, it deals more with how believers can live through crisis situations that bring untold suffering to people. It repeatedly points out that even though hardships, extreme difficulties, and cataclysmic events are "signs" of what is to come, they do not necessarily mean that the end is near because nobody really knows the time (vv. 3–7, 21, 32–33). Instead, what is underscored is the Christian's continuing outlook in times of great suffering, persecution, and confusion, which affect even those from the faith community. It describes how to live during the long span of time between the present life in this world, marked by periods of grave suffering, and the life to come, marked by the revelation of the glory of Christ that brings a halt to all suffering.

The Christian response is emphasized in repeated imperatives: Beware, keep alert (*blepete*, vv. 5, 23, 33) and "keep awake, keep watch" (*gregoreite*, vv. 35, 37), as well as in a participle that expresses one's continuing attitude in the midst of hardship—to be enduring, standing firm (*hupomeinas*)—and in a subjunctive form of the verb "to see, to perceive" (*idēte* vv. 14, 29), which calls attention to the "signs" that point to the Lord's coming. Thus, the movement of the whole chapter is towards the vindication of the Son of Man and the revelation of his glory.

The first basic stance in living in the in-between is *attentiveness*. This is emphasized in the subjunctive use of the verb "to see," "to perceive." We are being called to read the "signs" of God's presence and working in our midst. Attentiveness involves both spiritual and social discernment. Through prayer and careful listening to God's word, we seek to perceive what God is telling us through this catastrophe—this is spiritual discernment. But even as we listen to the cries of the world, we also seek to understand the factors that have caused the vulnerable to suffer more. This calls for social discernment—a careful reading of what is going on in society so that we can respond in appropriate ways in relation to what God has called us to be and to do.

The second attitude that is repeatedly emphasized is *vigilance*, as underlined in the repeated exhortation to "beware," "keep alert," and to "keep watch, keep awake," which are all in the imperative form. The liminal experience, while the source of new possibilities, is also a very fragile place. The dissolution of previous structures to enter into a state of ambiguity, emptiness, and uncertainty can be taken advantage of by others with a self-serving agenda, or whose vision of life is inimical to God.

Thus, in Mark 13, the call to vigilance, first of all, has to do with false messiahs who offer false promises of hope (vv. 21–22). They can claim to have the answers to the crisis, or guarantee stability, certainty and order, and may even present themselves as the voice of reason or the voice of God (v. 5) "to lead astray, if possible, the elect" (v. 22). Hence, there is a need to be alert and discerning, so as not to be lured away by deceptive and/or instant solutions, just because we want to have an easy and quick escape from all the suffering.

The Philippine government, for example, sees the spread of the virus as due to the Filipinos' lack of discipline, and thus its solution centers on militaristic approaches, rather than on proactive health measures and plans to deal with the economic fall-out of lockdown, especially on the marginalized. Thus, harsh punishments for minor violations of quarantine are exacted—you can be thrown into a crowded detention center for not wearing a mask, which in turn puts you more at risk of catching the virus. And of further concern, the passage of an Anti-Terror Law, whose provisions are akin to the Marcos's Martial Law, was given priority in Congress. The problem, however, is that the virus cannot be put under martial law. And so, even though the Philippines has one of the longest and strictest lockdowns in the world, the COVID-19 cases in the country continue to surge.

Another area of vigilance is to guard against complacency or laxity in terms of the task that God has called us to do. The metaphor for this is "sleeping," instead of "keeping awake" (vv. 33–37).

Especially during the lockdowns, when our normal life is suspended, it is easy to be paralyzed and to let it all go and lapse into laziness. We are not being asked to go beyond our own limitations, and there are many in a pandemic situation, but rather to be faithful to the daily tasks, no matter how boring and tiresome and restricted they seem to be.

The third theme in Mark 13 is *endurance*—to "stand firm"—the participle form of *hupomeinas*, showing a continuing attitude in the midst of hardship. The suffering may be prolonged, it may become worse, long-lasting, and pervasive. The people of God are not exempt from suffering. Rather, we are invited to embrace the suffering, even if it may have been the consequences of, or aggravated by, the failings of our religious and political leaders. This does not mean that we do not protest against unjust policies. But it does mean that, like Jesus, we are willing to bear the consequences of faulty decisions as part of the corporate body, and be committed to help shield the vulnerable from the impact of such decisions. "Staying in the pain," rather than moving quickly to a "new normal," expresses this stance of endurance.

Lastly, there is *hope* in a future marked by the revelation of the glory of Christ that brings a halt to the intense suffering. This does not necessarily mean the final end, but in every crisis, there is always a time when the suffering wanes and we catch a new vision of who God is amidst all the suffering. I do not know what this new vision would look like, for in order for hope and imagination to take place, we first still need to die. The resurrection—new life—comes only after the cross.

A Vigil in Times of Tragedy and Injustice[1]

Raising Our Voice on Behalf of the Voiceless

Charles Ringma

All: We will wait for the Lord. Our soul waits. And in God's word do we hope.

Reader: "For God alone my soul waits in silence; from him comes my salvation. God alone is my rock and my salvation, my fortress. I shall never be shaken" (Ps 62:1).

All: "We wait for the Lord, our soul waits. And in God's word do we hope. Our soul waits for the Lord more than those who watch for the morning, more than those who watch for the morning" (Ps 130:5–6).

Reader: "So now, O Israel, what does the Lord your God require of you? Only to fear the Lord your God, to walk in all his ways, to love him, and to serve the Lord your God with all your heart and with all your soul" (Deut 10:12).

All: We will wait for the Lord. Our soul waits. And in God's word do we hope.

Reader: "And he (Jesus) said to him: You shall love the Lord your God with all your heart, and with all your soul, and with all your mind. This is the

1. This liturgy has drawn material from *Celtic Daily Prayer*.

greatest and first commandment. And a second is like it: You shall love your neighbor as yourself" (Matt 22:37–39).

All: We will wait for the Lord. Our soul waits. And in God's word do we hope.

Reflective Music

All: Lord, we have heard your voice calling. Keep our heart for you, Lord. Keep our heart for you. Lord, we have heard your voice calling.

Reader: "When an alien resides with you in your land you shall not oppress the alien. The alien who resides with you shall be to you as the citizen among you. You shall love the alien as yourself, for you were aliens in the land of Egypt. I am the Lord your God" (Lev 19:33–34).

All: Lord, we have heard your voice calling. Keep our heart for you, Lord. Keep our heart for you. Lord, we have heard your voice calling.

Reader: "You shall not deprive a resident alien or an orphan of justice. You shall not take a widow's garment in pledge. Remember that you were a slave in Egypt and the Lord your God redeemed you from there; therefore I command you to do this" (Deut 24:17).

All: Lord, we have heard your voice calling. Keep our heart for you, Lord. Keep our heart for you. Lord, we have heard your voice calling.

Reader: "I know that the Lord maintains the cause of the needy and executes justice for the poor" (Ps 140:12).

All: Lord, we have heard your voice calling. Keep our heart for you, Lord. Keep our heart for you. Lord, we have heard your voice calling.

Reader: "People were bringing little children to him in order that he might touch them, and the disciples spoke sternly to them. But when Jesus saw this he was indignant and said to them: Let the little children come to me and do not stop them for it is to such that the kingdom of God belongs" (Mark 10:13–14).

All: Lord, we have heard your voice calling. Keep our heart for you, Lord. Keep our heart for you. Lord, we have heard your voice calling.

Reflective Music

All: Our Father in heaven, hallowed be your name. Your kingdom come, your will be done on earth as in heaven. Give us today our daily bread. Forgive us our sins as we forgive those who sin against us. Save us from the time of trial and deliver us from evil. For the kingdom, the power, and the glory are yours now and forever. Amen.

> *[Time of silent prayer for the government, for our medical personnel, for all who are responding to this crisis, for those most impacted by this crisis, particularly the poor and marginalized, and for ourselves, and the responses we are called to make].*

Reflective Music

All: Circle us, Lord. Keep protection near. And danger afar.

Reader: "Here is my servant, whom I uphold my chosen in whom my soul delights. I have put my spirit upon him, he will bring forth justice to the nations. He will not cry out or lift his voice, or make it heard in the street, a bruised reed he will not break, and a dimly burning wick he will not quench. He will faithfully bring forth justice" (Isa 42:1–4).

All: Circle us, Lord. Keep light near. And darkness afar.

Reader: "Seek the Lord while he may be found, call upon him while he is near. Let the wicked forsake their way and the unrighteous their thoughts. Let them return to the Lord that he may have mercy on them, and to our God, for he will abundantly pardon" (Isa 55:6–7).

All: Circle us, Lord. Keep peace within. Keep evil out.

Reader: "He shall judge between many peoples and shall arbitrate between strong nations far away. They shall beat their swords into plowshares and their spears into pruning hooks. Nation shall not lift up sword against nation neither shall they learn war anymore. But they shall sit under their own vines and under their own fig trees, and no one shall make them afraid for the mouth of the Lord has spoken" (Mic 4:3–4).

All: Circle us, Lord. Keep protection near. And danger afar.

Reflective Music

All: Our dear ones, O God, bless thou, and keep in every place where they are.

Reader: "Shamefully . . . some have been sent to detention camps offshore and uncounted others have been forced back to the homelands from where they have fled persecution before even being given a fair chance to tell their story and have their claim of asylum justly processed."[2]

All: Our dear ones, O God, bless thou and keep in every place where they are.

Reader: "Like any other children, unaccompanied children also have a range of rights that are protected under the *Children Rights Convention.* This includes rights to physical and mental health, education, culture, language, religion, rest, play, protection from violence, and to remain with their parents or to be reunited when separated."[3]

All: Our dear ones, O God, bless thou and keep in every place where they are.

Reader: In this time of crisis and tragedy may all governmental, medical, social welfare agencies, and community, and religious groups be mobilized to work cooperatively for the common good.

All: Our dear ones, O God, bless thou and keep in every place where they are.

Reader: In this time of great distress may special help be extended to all who are the most vulnerable in our society.

Reflective Music

All: In the shadow of your wings we will sing your praises, O Lord.

Reader: "The Son of God be shielding us with might. The Son of God be shielding us with power. May God free us from every entrapment. May God free us from every gully, from every torturous road."[4]

2. Australian Churches Refugee Taskforce, "Protecting the Lonely Children."
3. Australian Churches Refugee Taskforce, "Protecting the Lonely Children."
4. de Waal, ed., *The Celtic Vision*, 165–66.

All: In the shadow of your wings we will sing your praises, O Lord.

Reader: "Jesus, as a mother you gather your people to you; you are gentle with us as a mother with her children. Often you weep over our sins and our pride, tenderly you draw us from hatred and judgment. You comfort us in sorrow and bind up our wounds; in sickness you nurse us; and with pure milk you feed us. Jesus by your dying we are born to new life, by your anguish and labor we come forth in joy."[5]

All: In the shadow of your wings we will sing your praises, O Lord.

Reader: "Heal our inner sight, O God that we may know the difference between good and evil. Open our eyes that we may see what is true and what is false. Restore us to wisdom that we may be well in our own souls. Restore us to wisdom that we and our world may be well."[6]

All: In the shadow of your wings we will sing your praises, O Lord.

Reflective Music

All: Let our prayer rise before you as incense, and the lifting up of our hands as the day's sacrifice.

Reader: Jesus Christ is waiting, waiting in the streets. No one is his neighbor; all alone he eats. Listen, Lord Jesus, I am lonely too. Make me friend or stranger fit to wait for you.

All: Let our prayer rise before you as incense, and the lifting up of our hands as the day's sacrifice.

Reader: Jesus Christ is raging, raging in the streets where injustice spirals and real hope retreats. Listen, Lord Jesus, I am angry too. In the kingdom's causes let me rage with you.

All: Let our prayer rise before you as incense, and the lifting up of our hands as the day's sacrifice.

Reader: Jesus Christ is healing, healing in the streets, curing those who suffer, touching those he meets. Listen, Lord Jesus, I have pity too. Let my care be active healing just like yours.

5. Society of St. Francis, *Celebrating Common Prayer*, 232.
6. Newell, *Celtic Treasure*, 114.

All: Let our prayer rise before you as incense, and the lifting of our hands as the day's sacrifice.

Reader: Jesus Christ is calling, calling in the streets. Who will join my journey? I will guide their feet. Listen, Lord Jesus, let my tears be few. Walk one step before me. I will follow you.[7]

All: Let our prayer rise before you as incense, and the lifting of our hands as the day's sacrifice.

Reflective Music

All: In the tender compassion of our God the dawn from on high will break upon us.

Sayings from Martin Luther King, Jr.[8]

Reader: "I still have a dream that one day justice will roll down like water and righteousness like a mighty stream."

All: In the tender compassion of our God, the dawn from on high will break upon us.

Reader: The one "who loves is a participant in the being of God."

All: In the tender compassion of our God, the dawn from on high will break upon us.

Reader: "We are called to speak for the weak, for the voiceless, for victims of our nation, and for those it calls [an] enemy."

All: In the tender compassion of our God, the dawn from on high will break upon us.

Reader: "Non-cooperation with evil is as much a moral obligation as is cooperation with the good."

All: In the tender compassion of our God, the dawn from on high will break upon us.

7. Milgate, ed., *Together in Song*, 665.

8. Ringma, *Let My People Go with Martin Luther King, Jr.*

Reader: "Meet your physical force with soul force."

All: In the tender compassion of our God, the dawn from on high will break upon us.

Reflective Music

All: Blessed are the poor in spirit for theirs is the kingdom of heaven.

Blessed are those who mourn for they will be comforted.

Blessed are the meek for they will inherit the earth.

Blessed are those who hunger and thirst for righteousness for they will be filled.

Blessed are the merciful for they will receive mercy.

Blessed are the peacemakers for they will be called the children of God.

Blessed are those who are persecuted for righteousness' sake for theirs is the kingdom of heaven (Matt 5:1–10).

Reflective silence

All: Light a candle in the darkness, light a candle in the night.

Sayings of Thomas Merton[9]

Reader: "As long as we are on earth, the love that unites us will bring us suffering by our very contact with one another, because this love is the re-setting of a Body of broken bones."

All: Light a candle in the darkness, light a candle in the night.

Reader: "When we extend our hand to the enemy who is sinking in the abyss, God reaches out for both of us."

All: Light a candle in the darkness, light a candle in the night.

9. Ringma, *Seek the Silences with Thomas Merton.*

Reader: "You must be willing . . . to become a disturbing person, one who is not wanted because he [she] upsets the general dream."

All: Light a candle in the darkness, light a candle in the night.

Reader: "God is to be heard, not only on Sinai, not only in our own heart, but in the voice of the stranger."

All: Light a candle in the darkness, light a candle in the night.

Reader: "The monk [and we too] is essentially someone who takes up a critical attitude towards the world and its structures."

All: Light a candle in the darkness, light a candle in the night.

Reflective Music

Reader: We hear voices calling for a more humane, caring, and just social order.

All: Call forth more voices, O God.

Reader: We hear voices calling for more than only economic recovery.

All: Call forth more voices, O God.

Reader: We hear voices calling for the recovery of wounded planet earth.

All: Call forth more voices, O God.

Reader: We hear voices calling for greater shalom for the poor and the marginalized.

All: Call forth more voices, Lord.

Reflective Music

Reader: We don't know how to change some present government policy.

All: Hear our prayer, O Lord.

Reader: We don't know how to advocate well.

All: Give us and others wisdom, O God.

Reader: We don't know how to mobilize our churches and communities.

All: Hear our cry, O Lord.

Reader: We don't know how to love our neighbor well.

All: Christ have mercy.

Reflective Music

Reader: God of mercy and justice, we confess that we have not loved you with our whole heart.

All: Christ have mercy.

Reader: God of love, we confess that we have not loved our neighbor as ourselves.

All: Christ have mercy.

Reader: God of welcome, we confess that we have closed our hearts and eyes to the poor at our doorstep.

All: Lord, have mercy.

Reader: God of compassion, we confess that we are self-centered and self-preoccupied.

All: Christ have mercy.

Reader: God of tenderness, we can confess that we have not been passionate about the vulnerable and needy.

All: Lord, have mercy.

All: Lord, we are sorry for our sins of commission and omission, and for the sins of our nation. We repent in humility of heart. We ask for your forgiveness. We pray that you will renew us and empower us to serve you, the God of justice, to advocate on behalf of the needy and to accompany them to newness of life. Amen.

Reflective Music

All: Christ, as a light illumine and guide us. Christ, as a shield overshadow us.

Christ under us. Christ over us. Christ beside us on our left and our right.

This day be within and without us, lowly and meek, yet all powerful.

Be in the heart of each to whom we speak; in the mouth of each who speaks unto us.

This day be within and without us, lowly and meek, yet all powerful.

Christ as a light, Christ as a shield, Christ beside us on our left and our right.[10]

All: In the name of the Father, and of the Son, and of the Holy Spirit. Amen

10. Northumbria Community, *Celtic Daily Prayer*, 18–19.

Here is my servant whom I have chosen,

the one I love, in whom I delight;

I will put my Spirit on him, and he will proclaim
justice to the nations . . .

In his name the nations will put
their hope (Matt 12:18–21).

Lord, in the death and resurrection of Jesus Christ

you have given us hope both for this world and the world to come.

We choose to trust you, for our individual lives and for our nations.

We look for your reign of justice, righteousness,

and peace that will come in its fullness.

11

Hope in a World in Crisis: A Reflection

Sarah Nicholl

> The Beatitudes are one of the great promises of Christ and his new covenant. They are the promise as a lifestyle. Once again, this promise begins in the present . . . But the reign will only be manifested fully and forever in the future life. This is what we hope for. Christian hope is to live now already, in the invisible realm of faith, what we will see one day face to face.—Segundo Galilea, *A Spirituality of Hope*[1]

C. S. Lewis in the Narnia series created an imaginary world where the never-ending winter turns to spring in the presence of Aslan, the lion. Aslan, who is both wild and compassionate; whose eyes penetrate others and overwhelm; a lion who is willing to die for Edward, "the son of man" addicted to turkish delight and giving his allegiance to the evil Queen; Aslan, who is subsequently resurrected to live in and for Narnia.[2] For some, this story is a children's myth of adventure, but for others, with the insight of the biblical narratives, they see Lewis's crafting of a theological landscape that speaks to his readers of a God who is immanent and transcendent, who never fails to take care of the world. In Narnia, Aslan is Lewis's picture of Jesus, one who is present in the world today through the Holy Spirit.

For me, Narnia is a picture of hope, a place where God's values and truth are reigning. I like Lewis's metaphor of the wardrobe as the means

1. Galilea, *A Spirituality of Hope*, 6.
2. Lewis, *The Lion, the Witch, and the Wardrobe.*

of entry to Narnia. This large wooden object, common in most bedrooms, a place to keep our clothes, is transformed. Lewis turns this functional, ordinary, and practical closet into a mysterious place of transition from one world to another. For me, the wardrobe is an icon.

When I asked my fifteen-year-old son, "What's an icon?" He laughed at me: "Mum, it is a symbol on a computer screen representing a digital application." This was not the answer I was expecting. I was thinking of an ornate religious picture found often in Eastern Orthodox worship. I had to take a moment to rethink. A wardrobe, a digital symbol, a religious picture, all of them icons? I knew what the wardrobe and the ornate picture did, but the digital symbol, does this fit the same description? Maybe I misunderstood the term. I reviewed the word in a dictionary; my son's understanding was correct, but there were other definitions: religious symbol, image, and emblem. Not quite what I understood the word to mean, I did some further digging.

An article in *Loyola Press* affirmed my own thoughts. It noted that the religious icon as sacred art brought the viewer to the holy, that is, it was more than a symbol:

> Icons have been called windows to heaven or doorways to the sacred. When you are standing in front of an icon, it is as if you are looking through a window into the heavenly world of the mystery. But this is a two-way window. As you look through the window, you are also being seen with the eyes of love by those in the icon. It's like you become a part of the mystery that the icon seeks to express.[3]

My understanding of an icon is in keeping with this description. In Eastern Orthodox religion by contemplating a religious picture, often of Jesus, you are mysteriously transported into the reality of God's world. I consider this is what Lewis's wardrobe does; it transports those who enter it into Jesus' (Aslan's) kingdom.

The Apostle Matthew, in his record of the Sermon on the Mount, writes that Jesus tells his disciples not to pray in public for show, like the Pharisees, but to go to one's closet, inner room, basically a quiet place where no one can see you, and pray to your Father who is unseen, in secret (Matt 6:57). The wardrobe, a place of quiet, a space where no one can find you, a place to investigate, was what Lucy found in Lewis's novel. Yet this closet is one that can take you surprisingly into the presence of God.[4] Is this just an interesting

3. *Loyola Press*, "Icons as Religious Art."

4. Lewis, *The Lion, the Witch and the Wardrobe*, 6–7.

thought or is the wardrobe, as an icon or place of prayer, a functional tool? Do we have these wardrobes or closets in our lives?

The current pandemic affects all of us around the globe. For once, everyone has something in common. To one extent or another, we are all imprisoned within our homes, our towns, countries. Our neighbors must physically distance themselves two meters or six feet away from us. We cannot hug or shake hands; human touch is forbidden. Family ties are challenged, grandparents are separated from grandchildren, and parents from children who are not living at home. Everything that is taken for granted is upturned. Despair and depression are rising as we are starved of an important part of our lives: safe love in community.

I dream of freedom, of wandering through my wardrobe into Narnia, where I can observe children playing with Aslan, riding on his back, rolling in long grass, having fun. It is a good place to go, a place to encounter God. However, the question I ask myself is this: what I am called to do? Am I only to contemplate and thereby remove myself from reality? Narnia as a metaphorical space is not an escape from the world; for me, it is a place of contemplation, where I perceive what life might be like if all persons accepted Christ's reign, not just in their personal lives but in the world. I think if I truly entered Narnia and Aslan's penetrating eyes caught mine, it would not be long before I found myself back in the wardrobe and in the reality of my life. My reentry would not be out of fear of Aslan but out of a realization of love. If I meet the person who gave so much for me, do I not want to reciprocate by doing that to which God calls me?

Saint Paul knew what it was to live in challenging circumstances. He wrote to the Corinthian church: "We are hard pressed on every side, but not crushed; perplexed but not in despair; persecuted but not abandoned; struck down but not destroyed" (2 Cor 4:8–9—all Bible references in this chapter are from the NIV). He experienced danger, hate, and imprisonment, but through it all, he rested in Christ. He could say, "when I am weak, then I am strong" (2 Cor 12:10). He retained hope in the one whom he had encountered on the road to Damascus and who had done so much for him.

As I write, the last few months have brought challenges into our world that most of us have not experienced before. We have seen governments struggle to come to terms with the reality of the virus. Some have been overwhelmed. Others have used it to grab power, while yet others have coped admirably. I live in the province of British Columbia in Canada, where I have experienced little of the devastating effects that I have seen through the media. British Columbia has weathered the storm well, thanks in part to an experienced Provincial Health Officer, Dr. Bonnie Henry. She gained the people's trust early and consequently, most of the population of this province obeyed her directions, with enviable results. Other provinces such as Ontario and Quebec have not fared so well. In Canada, about 20,000 persons have died from COVID-19 to date. Each person either a grandparent, mother, father, son, daughter, aunt, uncle, or cousin of someone. The effects are much broader than those who have died or who are ill.

At the same time, I am also seeing the immense pressure to return to normality. Our economies are suffering and there is a push to go back to work, to buy and sell. This conflict is seen particularly in the US, where many states want to resume commercial endeavors even if it means the sacrifice of lives. Today, we are seeing spikes in the numbers contracting the virus in states such as Arizona, Florida, and California, which professionals consider opened too early. The reality of the human tragedy came home to me when I saw the many caskets of dead bodies being placed in huge public graves in New York and Brazil—a horror that is not easy to dismiss.

What, as Christians, can we do? How can we make a difference? How can we love our neighbor? Many churches are joining with other groups to make meals for the essential workers on the front lines, who risk their lives for us. We give money to those in need, who have lost jobs and cannot pay their rent. There are many practical things both large and small that we can and should do. However, I am struck by many people's lack of hope, the fear of death, and an unknown future.

Saint Peter in his first epistle exhorts his readers to give a reason for the hope that they have as Christians (1 Pet 3:15). I ask myself, am I filled with this hope so that others recognize it, and ask me about it? Or am I as fearful as my neighbor?

A person who has challenged and helped me often on my Christian journey is the late Father Segundo Galilea, a Chilean priest who lived and worked in South America, and died in 2010. While I never met the man, I have talked with colleagues who knew him, and I have read his many books.[5] I intend in this chapter to share some of his wisdom. In *A Spirituality of Hope*, he notes: "[Christian hope] changes the meaning of life,

5. I recommend Galilea, *The Way of Living Faith*; *Following Jesus*; and *The Beatitudes: To Evangelize as Jesus Did.*

our way of living, of dying, of acting, and the value we give to all things. Christian hope, like faith and charity, is incarnated in life."[6]

Christian hope transforms life as Christians live in the experience of it. It is not human hope even though such hope is often good. It is something different. The original Greek word in the New Testament for hope is *elpis*. It is translatable as hope, expectation and/or anticipation of good, trust, confidence. It is a positive word. Christians are called to live by faith in what God has promised to do. God has promised to restore all things to complete wholeness and Christians live in expectation that this will come to pass. God's reign of justice, righteousness, and peace will come in its fullness as Christ has redeemed all things, including Christians who have such faith in Christ (Col 1:15–20). In theological terms, this final event of God's complete restoration is termed the "eschaton." God's Holy Spirit abides in and with Christians affirming the truth of this promise (Eph 1:14). Thus, the Christian expectation of God's faithfulness to fulfill these promises is not a mere mental assent, but rather an expectation based on the inner promptings of the Spirit, who guarantees what is to come. It is faith in this confident hope that God will fulfill all God's promises that spurs the love of Christians into action.

The Bible is filled with stories of persons who live with such faith and hope in God's promises. The writer to the Hebrews lists a whole group of persons who lived in this way, and whose behavior and society was changed as a consequence (Heb 11). Abraham is one such person, whose faith and hope in God's promises led him to act swiftly and obediently. The book of Genesis records his story as a man who encounters God and is given both directions and promises; his response is to act immediately.

The Lord said to Abram, "Leave your country, your people and your father's household, and go the land I will show you. I will make you into a great nation, and I will bless you; I will make your name great, and you will be a blessing. I will bless those who bless you, and whoever curses you I will curse; and all the peoples of the earth will be blessed through you" (Gen 12:13).

The writer to the Hebrews also notes that "*faith* is being *sure* of what we *hope* for and *certain* of what we do not see" (Heb 11:1, emphasis mine). Christian hope in God's faithfulness grounds faith and should encourage us to act. After the above-mentioned promise to Abraham is recorded, the next verse states: "So Abram left." He did not question or delay. At the age of

6. Galilea, *A Spirituality of Hope*, 8.

seventy-five he packed up all that he had, his family, his household, and left Haran for Canaan. By trusting that God would keep his promises, Abraham was obedient to God's request. He did this even when God asked him to sacrifice his son Isaac whom God had also promised would be the source of Abraham's offspring. Abraham still believed that God would keep the promise: "he reasoned that God could raise the dead" (Heb 11:19). Abraham is commended as a man of faith because he did not doubt that God would keep his promises even in dire circumstances, and he acted as though they were already fulfilled. Abraham's actions were his hope incarnated.

The Bible is filled with God's promises to God's people. Jesus' life, death, and resurrection inaugurated the start of some of these through God's provision of salvation and the inauguration of God's kingdom in the present. Consequently, while we live in a liminal time between the "now" and the "not yet," many of these pledges are at least in part realizable now. In other words, Christians are already blessed with some of the benefits of these promises today.

Father Galilea argues that the Beatitudes are some of God's promises, pledges to us about Christ and God's kingdom values.[7] Blessed are the merciful for they shall be shown mercy (Matt 5:7). Jesus is the merciful one and God's kingdom is one of mercy. Blessed are the pure in heart for they will see God (Matt 5:8). Jesus was pure in heart and he saw and communicated with God. Blessed are the peacemakers for they will be called sons of God (Matt 5:9). Jesus was a peacemaker and he was truly the Son of God. However, while Christians can hope for this future, they can also partially realize some of this truth now.

Christians experience God's mercy today and are called to extend mercy to others. Christians mourn and they know God's comfort. Then they are called to bear witness to this comfort. Christians are called to become like the human Jesus, and in becoming so, they are able to envisage God, even if obscurely. Further, our call is not necessarily an individual one or a solitary one. God does not ask Christians to do this alone. Jesus promised and sent the Holy Spirit to enable us, direct us, and participate with the Spirit in such tasks. It is not in our own strength that we can do these things, but through the power of the Holy Spirit who dwells with and in us. Paul stated in his letter to the Galatians: "I have been crucified with Christ and I no longer live, *but Christ lives in me.* The life I live in the body, I live by faith in the Son of

7. Galilea, *The Beatitudes: To Evangelize as Jesus Did*, 8–9.

God who loved me, and gave himself for me" (Gal 2:20, emphasis mine). It is through God's Spirit in us that Christians live.

In God's design we also have the fellowship of other Christians. The Christian church as the community of God's people is called to live together in unity and work together to represent God's kingdom to the world. Again, Jesus promises where "two or three come together in my name, there am I, with them" (Matt 18:20). Therefore, even in this difficult time, we must try to do all we can as community. Even if I pray alone, I can remember that I am praying with many Christians all around the globe.

Christian hope is built both on the future and the now. Galilea argues that as Christians are called to live their hope, they should also look for "the seeds of the future in the present."[8] In other words, our God, who does not slumber or sleep, is at work in our world through the Holy Spirit. Therefore, if I attend to the world, I will see glimpses that can encourage me in my Christian hope.

In this time of isolation, one thing that gives me hope is that despite all the challenges, nature and time continue. I have watched how in the northern hemisphere spring has turned to summer. The birds came out on time and in chorus. The daffodils and tulips bloomed. Lilac breathed its heavenly scent, and now roses and lavender blossom and feed bees. The sun rises in the sky every morning and bids farewell every night. Light and good things abound in our world, despite it all. For me, God is saying, I am still here.

You may be asking at this point, what has all of this to do with Narnia, wardrobes, the current pandemic? For me, it is this: our neighbors need hope, they need to see Christian hope. Human hope in a vaccine can no doubt overcome some of their fears. However, if my neighbors could experience Christian hope incarnated in me, surely they would see a difference. Christians have a hope in something that is unseen but real. In order to live this out, I believe I must find the icons or windows into God's world, where I now have time to stay awhile and contemplate God and God's promises.

As I write this, I realize that sometimes the closet is a difficult place to be. If I close the door, it is dark and can be oppressive. However, like Lucy who discovered light in her dark place, one that guided her to Narnia, I know that so will I, if I persist.[9] I do believe that as a Christian I must attend to God before I can go out into the world and do God's bidding.

8. Galilea, *A Spirituality of Hope*, 56.

9. Lewis, *The Lion, the Witch, and the Wardrobe*, 8.

I must know God's voice and will before I act. I must, in my closet, encounter Jesus though the Holy Spirit and come to know God so that I can recognize the Holy Spirit at work in God's world, and participate with God. I have to receive mercy, purity, peace to live out the Beatitudes and reveal God's kingdom to others. But as I said at the beginning, I believe that having encountered God, I will quickly find myself with directions, empowerment, and love to act through the Holy Spirit. As I act, I also know I will discover my need to return to my wardrobe, to relate to God, to enable God's strength to fill my weakness, for refreshment, and a reminder of the hope that is God.

In this challenging time, there are no easy answers. My husband who is a senior executive in a large company tells me, "It is a time that requires innovation." My response is to tell him and myself to pray, not just to intercede but to contemplate. I know such comments can sound facile, but I do believe that God is the Creator and Innovator who will give help, if we ask and attend to God's voice.

Galilea recounts his visit to a high security prison in Manila, in the Philippines, with a fellow nun and the wife of a prisoner, John, to celebrate Holy Communion for John and his wife's wedding anniversary. Galilea notes that most of the prisoners were political. John was a lawyer and a journalist, and had been resident in the prison for nine years. While visiting, Galilea was struck by two things: the well-being of the prisoners (they were relaxed and amiable), and the religious atmosphere of the prison: Christian symbols and Gospel sayings adorned the walls. There were no locks on the doors and prisoners were able to move around freely. The prison guards were also friendly.

John told Galilea of his time in the prison. He explained how he had spent the first two years in solitary confinement and had used this time to write, read Scripture, pray, review his life, and deepen his faith. After this, he became busy. He helped other prisoners write letters and judiciary appeals, many of them receiving reduced sentences. With the help of other inmates, he also started several prayer and Bible study groups. The impact for Galilea was significant. This was like no other security prison he had visited. Many more persons attended the communion than he expected, and it became clear as prisoners participated and sang songs that this was a regular event.

Of the experience, Galilea states that "hope had acquired for me a new and tangible reality. Very seldom before had I been able to 'hear, touch and see' hope as I did at that moment." These prisoners were forgotten, with no expectations of release. The condition of the prison itself was dehumanizing and no human hope was identifiable. John had cause to be depressed, empty, and bitter. However, instead he had chosen to live with Christian hope. He lived by what he did not see and chose to love and serve others.[10] After narrating his experience, Galilea notes: "Hope flourishes when it is practiced, when one acts as if its promises were real."[11]

I live in a challenging world, a strange new society in which I am trying to navigate new protocols and new ways of being and acting. In such times, it is good to be reminded of the hope that I have as a Christian, to go to my wardrobe and visit Narnia, to trust and be confident in the Triune God, to know that God is faithful, just, and always the same. Moreover, it is here that I can learn, with the person of the Holy Spirit, how to practice this hope and incarnate the ethos of the Beatitudes to the challenged neighborhood in which I live.

10. Galilea, *A Spirituality of Hope*, 50–53.

11. Galilea, *A Spirituality of Hope*, 54.

Prayer in Times of Crisis

Charles Ringma with prayers by
Paul Mercer and Ross McKenzie

The heart of Christianity is people impacted by the gospel through the Spirit and seeking to live in the way of Christ and in service to the neighbor. For most, the gathered church is vital as a source of sustenance and on-going formation, as well as the place for combined missional activity. The time of pandemic has brought into question what changes there may be in churches and communities of faith—not just first-order changes like on-line services, but second-order changes—change in terms of a significant paradigm shift.

But however the above may unfold, we need most fundamentally to be a people of prayer! Martin Luther wrote: "Prayer is the chief work of the Christian."[1] Prayer not only renews our life with God and blesses the church, but, importantly, according to Luther, prayer "can preserve the world."[2] We have the example of "prayer warriors" of the past who exemplified this, including the desert fathers and mothers. These Christians went into the desert to pray for a renewed church and world. It was second-order change that they sought. And they did so as a lay movement. They were concerned that the church of their day had become too culturally captive. And they believed that through prayer and ascetic practices, a revitalized

1. Luther, *Luther's Works*, vol. 21, 228.
2. Luther, *Luther's Works*, vol. 24, 80.

church could come into being. As such, these desert Christians were the forebears of monasticism, which played such an essential part in the further development of Christianity.

What might be the "deserts" we need to inhabit and in which we could pray for a renewed church? And what prayer commitments are we called to for God's kingdom to break through more fully in our world? Might we find prayerful solidarity with those of the poor and most dispossessed who carry the most substantial weight of the current social upheaval and crisis? And in such a desert place might we become more fully attuned to the movements of the Spirit of Christ as we discern the seeds of second-order change that the Spirit is planting. Will this bring comfort to the oppressed, renew our life with God, revive and bless the church, and preserve our world?

To be a people of prayer is to pray. Rather than speak more of prayer, our proposal for the remainder of this chapter is to offer several responsive prayers that might guide you to your desert place in this time of crisis.

Prayer of Lament

In a recent article in *Time* magazine, N. T. Wright argues that the most appropriate response of Christians to the COVID-19 pandemic is lament. "Lament is what happens when people ask, 'Why?' and don't get an answer. It's where we get to when we move beyond our self-centered worry about our sins and failings and look more broadly at the suffering of the world."[1] In the psalms of lament, the writers passionately express their grief and questioning in response to tragedy and suffering.

Reflect on Psalm 13:

> I'm hurting, Lord—will you forget me forever?
>
> How much longer, Lord? Will you look the other way when I'm in need?
>
> How much longer must I cling to this constant grief? I've endured this shaking of my soul.
>
> So how much longer will my enemy have the upper hand? It's been long enough!
>
> Take a good look at me, God, and answer me! Breathe your life into my spirit.

1. Wright, "Christianity Offers No Answers About the Coronavirus."

> Bring light to my eyes in this pitch-black darkness or I will sleep the sleep of death.
>
> Don't let my enemy proclaim, "I've prevailed over him." For all my adversaries will celebrate when I fall.
>
> Lord, I have always trusted in your kindness, so answer me. I will yet celebrate with passion and joy when your salvation lifts me up.
>
> I will sing my song of joy to you, the Most High, for in all of this you have strengthened my soul.
>
> My enemies say that I have no Savior, but I know that I have one in you! (Ps 13 TPT)

Besides some of the psalms, another example is the book of Lamentations. "These laments are a form of protest, a way of processing emotion, as well as a place to voice confusion. Suffering makes us ask questions about God's character and none of this is looked down on in the Bible. These words give a sacred dignity to human suffering . . . Lament, prayer, and grief are a crucial part of the journey of faith of God's people in a broken world."[2]

Eugene Peterson also notes that lament is essential: "A failure to lament is a failure to connect . . . We're in a story in which everything eventually comes together, a narrative in which all the puzzling parts finally fit, about which years later we exclaim, 'Oh, so that's what that meant!' But being in a story means that we mustn't attempt to get ahead of the plot—skip the hard parts, erase the painful parts, detour the disappointments."[3] Lament, he notes, is making the most of our loss without getting bogged down in it. It is a primary way of staying in the story, staying honest to our reality.

Jesus identified with the lament of Psalm 22 while dying on the cross: "My God, my God, why have you forsaken me?"

[Time of silence to write or speak one's own lament.]

2. Lamentations Bible Project.

3. Peterson, *Leap Over a Wall*, 121.

Praying Together in Pandemic

Leader: God of love and peace, be with us in our worship today.

People: From the beginning you have been the creator of our cosmos. Your spirit hovering over chaos has gifted beauty and life.

Leader: Creator God, we look into your face and confess our need of the breath of the Spirit.

People: Good creator, be with us in our time of pandemic crisis and fear. Restore the holy kiss of grace to us. The whole world is in your hands.

Leader: God of love and peace, be with us in our worship today.

People: Lord of light and starfields deep. Lord of earth and water gathered to seas, flatten the chaos of plague and racial distress in this day. Protect your people off- and online.

Leader: We give thanks for the warmth of sun, the wild beauty of every living thing. Enable the stewardship of your image in us today. In crisis, we need your grace to sustain us in the ministry of reconciliation. We thank you for indigenous peoples, the historical custodians of this land.

People: The smell of death, your breath removed is a great distress in our time. Remember your good creation, Adam's race; your promise to be with us until the end of this age.

Leader: God of love and peace, be with us in our worship today.

People: We praise you for the blessing of life itself, and thank you that in times of doubt you draw near to us. You commission us with salvation joy. The agency of gospel is reconciliation.

Leader: O Lord, our Lord, how majestic is your name in all the earth. Through the self-giving love of your Son and the baptizing presence of your Spirit, be with us in all our days. We are your witnesses.

People: We confess the challenge of caring for and "ruling over" the works of your hands in a world broken by economic disruption, environmental stress, food security, and our peoples' health in chaos. We are struggling to love one another through social and mental health distress. In repentance, we seek your salvation, O God. You alone are our glory and honor.

All: Good creator, Lord of heaven and earth, Father, Son, and Spirit with us. Our world needs to hear again the encouragement of your love and peace. Graciously restore our harmony in this strange time of distancing. May the fellowship of Father, Son, and Holy Spirit embrace us all in love, today and forevermore. Amen.

[Drawn from Genesis 1, Psalm 8, Matthew 28, 2 Corinthians 12:11–14.]

Prayer of Intercession

Leader: Our Father, we come with confidence into your presence. We call out, "Tilt your ears towards us now. Listen to our prayer."

People: For your faithful love, we are thankful. We need you to save in this day of pandemic threat. Show your love in amazing ways. Hear the fevered cries for help. Make us vessels of relief and instruments of peace.

Leader: Red, yellow, black, and white—we are all precious in your sight. In Jesus, you are putting the world right. Let your eyes see the help we need.

People: Like Jacob, we are wrestling through the dark night of COVID-19. We know your name is Father, your name is Jesus the Son, your name is Spirit, the Comforter. Prepare us for change. Prepare us for the future as your reconciling people, your emissaries of grace.

Leader: Lord, in the light of your love, we want to see your face in our troubled times. We stand in solidarity with you and our world.

People: Jesus, fill us with your compassion for the sick. We pray for neighbors in New South Wales, Victoria, Papua New Guinea, India, South Sudan, and beyond. Bless public health officials, health, and aged care workers. Bless scientists diligent in searching for a vaccine. Lord, hear the cries for mercy of all in intensive care.

Leader: Jesus told his disciples, "You give them something to eat." So we pray for a Spirit-fired imagination and commitment to all who face food insecurity in this time of crisis. Bless anew our loaves and fishes today.

People: Our Father, who has always been a refuge to his children, by your strong hand protect the weak and vulnerable at this time. May the cross of Christ and his resurrection power be an anchor in this storm.

All: We bless you, Father, Son, and Spirit, for our heritage in your new creation. Cause our hearts to burn in love for all our neighbors. Fill us with the vision of your glory. Our song of praise is to the Son who rules over all things. Together in Christ, we bless your name forever. Amen.

[Drawn from Genesis 32:22–32; Psalm 17:1–7, 15; Romans 9:1–5; Matthew 14:13–21.]

Prayer of Hope

Leader: God has gone up with a joyous shout.

People: We rise to join in praise to you.

Leader: Our God, Father, Son, and Spirit, is King over the nations.

People: In this time of the pandemic crisis we acknowledge that we are the earth's guardians.

Leader: God has gone up with a joyous shout.

People: Because you have placed everything under Christ's feet.

Leader: The one who washes our feet is the head of everything in the church.

People: Jesus our Lord, who gives us the Holy Spirit as the down-payment of resurrection life, release us from fear, strengthen our love for you, and energize the service to our neighbors in this time of distress.

Leader: God has gone up with a joyous shout.

People: From north, south, east, and west, we applaud your self-giving love in Jesus.

Leader: Our God, we cry for mercy for our world in this COVID plague. Remember to do us good.

People: We clap our hands as we recognize your awesome providence daily flowing in and though front-line healthcare workers, straining to keep your people alive. Sustain them, protect them from this viral evil. Give us all peace.

Leader: God has gone up with a joyous shout.

People: With joyful praise, we embrace the gift of your self-giving love, filling us and spreading all over the world in the Holy Spirit's power.

Leader: In this season of pandemic fear, ignite our imagination to serve in the power of the Spirit.

People: Help us become your hands and feet around the cries of economic distress, mental anguish, and personal brokenness.

Leader: God has gone up with a joyous shout.

People: Your grace has changed our hearts and forgiven our sins. May our lives be transformed by the way of the cross and the power of the resurrected Christ. Help us to be a witness in our world battered and on its knees.

Leader: Incarnate, crucified, resurrected Lord, we, your people, declare our hope is in you alone.

People: May the curve be flattened in every corner of the earth. May all people know you have provided their daily bread. May your wisdom in science shine its light on treatments for COVID-19 and bring immunity to the world.

All: May the grace and truth of the ascended glorified Son of God, and the fellowship of Father, Son, and Spirit in love, remain with us and embrace our world today and evermore. Amen. We shout for Joy!

[Drawn from Psalm 47; Ephesians 1:15–23; Luke 24:44–52; Acts 1:1–11.]

Appendix 1

Questions for Reflection and Discussion

Chapter 1: Welcoming Troubled Souls —Reflective Questions

"When Jesus came down from the mountainside, large crowds followed him. A man with leprosy came and knelt before him and said, 'Lord, if you are willing, you can make me clean.' Jesus reached out his hand and touched the man. 'I am willing,' he said. 'Be clean!' Immediately he was cleansed of his leprosy" (Matt 8:1–3 NIV). In this encounter, we witness the extremes of poverty: physical, material, relational, societal, and political. And yet this pilgrim knew, in his poverty of spirit, that Jesus had life for him.

1. How might an acknowledgment of our poverty of spirit in this time of crisis awaken us to the reality that Jesus has life for us?
2. If you were to place yourself in the above encounter between Jesus and this man, what would you notice about what is death-making and what is life-giving for you?
3. In what ways has your poverty of spirit been amplified in this time of crisis?
4. What awakens and stirs within you in the spacious presence of the Spirit?

Chapter 2: Mourning, Comfort and the "New Normal" —Reflective Questions

1. When in your life have you most strongly experienced a liminal space—the space when you have moved on from the past, but don't know yet what the future will be?
2. In what ways has the pandemic or another crisis been a liminal space for you?
3. In what ways have you become more prayerful, or more conscious of God, during times of crisis?
4. How have you experienced God's comfort when you are mourning your losses?
5. In what ways have you experienced *acedia*—the boredom or disengagement that comes with sameness?
6. How could you see the church responding to the challenge of a liminal space in this crisis-time?
7. In what ways have you become aware of God's kingdom realm growing in recent times?
8. The author describes crisis times as being in the womb of God. How do you resonate with this metaphor?

Chapter 3: Blessed are the Meek—Reflective Questions

1. Near the beginning of the chapter the author lists some truths that we struggle to accept. Which of these truths are hardest for you to accept?
2. Is there a difference between being humbled and the practice of humility?
3. Why do many of us find being unable to control aspects of our lives so humbling?
4. In what ways does being a good scientist require humility?
5. What do you think of John Dickson's definition of humility? How might you change it? Is there a biblical basis for his definition?
6. Do you agree or disagree that humility is more about "how I treat others than how I think about myself"? Why?

7. In the Genesis account of the fall, Adam and Eve were humbled. Did they gain humility? Why or why not?
8. How has a crisis such as COVID-19 humbled you or people you know? What have been the consequences in your life?
9. How are you more open to being dependent on others during a crisis? How about after a crisis?
10. How can the process of living through COVID-19 help us to reorder our thinking about life and make us stronger people?

Chapter 4: Jesus' Invitation to Vulnerability —Reflective Questions

1. In what ways have you found that this time of crisis has held up a mirror to you/your family/church or work?
2. In what ways have you sought for goodness and justice during this time?
3. What happens for you when you see the way of Jesus being the way of vulnerability?
4. In what ways is the image of God being vulnerable a familiar image to you? An uncomfortable image? A challenging image?
5. What is it like for you to contemplate this description of the true self as a living out of a vulnerable, unmasked place?
6. In what ways do you get tricked into being a Pharisee, or the older brother in the story of the prodigal son?
7. How have you been called to interdependence in your community and lifestyle?
8. In what ways are you caring for the vulnerable earth?
9. What lifestyle changes are you being invited into in this crisis and the call of the Sermon on the Mount?
10. How might Jesus' invitation to vulnerability shape your conceptualization of the "new normal"?

Chapter 5: Stay with Me. Watch and Pray. —Reflective Questions

1. What has been your experience of praying for others, and how has it shaped your understanding of intercession?
2. Who would you invite to stay with you when facing a crisis? What is it about these particular people that would help you in dealing with your crisis?
3. What resonates with your experience from this chapter? What does not resonate with your experience? What insights do these thoughts have for your practice of intercessory prayer or being merciful?
4. What have you personally learned about being present or staying with another when facing their crisis or difficulty? What has been important to keep in mind for you, as you seek to support them?
5. Think of a crisis you are facing, then ask yourself: "How would I want a friend to support me, or intercede for me, in this crisis?"
6. What does Jesus' admonition to his disciples to "watch and pray" suggest to you about being with and supporting one another in prayer?
7. What do you learn from Jesus' prayer (in Gethsemane) about how you might pray for yourself when facing a personal crisis?

Chapter 6: In-Christ, In Crisis—Reflective Questions

1. As a doctor, the author is impacted by COVID-19 in very specific ways. What are some specific ways this crisis has affected your life?
2. Rowan Williams says that we know God if we also experience "crucifying compassion." Reflect on where you may have experienced this in your life.
3. The author reflects on what it means to be pure in heart in the reality of daily life. Reflecting on your life, where are the invitations to be pure in heart?
4. David made many mistakes, but turned back to God, seeking a pure heart. He trusted God's forgiveness. What are the experiences that have taught you of God's forgiveness and a renewed invitation to purity of heart?

5. The eight deadly thoughts are gluttony, sexual sin, greed, anxiety, sadness, anger, apathy, vainglory, and pride. What caught your attention as you read this section?
6. We are reminded to imagine ourselves encountering the resurrected Jesus. What happens for you as you place yourself in this story?
7. The practices this chapter explores are prayer, engaging the Scriptures, and fellowship. What do these practices look like in your life?
8. Productivity is defined very broadly. Where might you see this in your own life?

Chapter 7: Guides for the Soul—Reflective Questions

1. How would it be for you to receive guidance like Bob? Have you experienced something similar?
2. Did you notice any heart resonance with Bob's experiences?
3. Has something been stirred within that you could take into your prayer, or into a conversation with your guide, mentor, or spiritual companion?
4. How has this chapter helped to extend your ways of guiding or companioning pilgrims, particularly in a time of crisis?
5. Is there something of this chapter you could take into a group of which you are part?

Chapter 8: In the World and Not Afraid —Reflective Questions

1. Augustine, Chrysostom, and Thomas à Kempis are all quoted as knowing that the Christian endures suffering, as Christ did. What happens for you as you reflect on this understanding?
2. In the section "When Crises Come" a number of historical disasters are listed, with the responses of Christians to these disasters. What inspired or moved you in this section?
3. Christians are in Christ and in the world, a dual citizenship. How in your life do you live this tension?

4. The author explores a number of responses to being in crisis: acknowledge our fears and anxieties; embrace loss; identify with the suffering God; wrestle in prayer; give practical help; seek justice; enter more deeply into the mystery of God. Which of these resonate with you in terms of your own response? Which can you see your church responding to? To which of these would you like to respond further?
5. In your group discuss how you might, as a group, respond to these invitations (from the previous question).

Chapter 9: Treasure in Heaven—Reflective Questions

1. In what ways has the economic results of the pandemic affected you personally, or those near you?
2. From your experience are economic decisions and policies more like a science, an art, or a knee-jerk reaction on the run?
3. How do you see yourself "fixing your attention on God" when it comes to economic questions and decisions?
4. Look again at the list of verses Benson refers to from Genesis, Malachi, Matthew, and Luke. In what ways do you see and use these verses as guiding principles in your life?
5. Similarly, what about the biblical principles he lists starting with "This is God's world and we are only tenants and temporary custodians"? Which of these are you familiar with? Which would you name as guiding principles in your economic decisions?
6. Benson explains "market failure" and how privatization has been a response to that. What is your understanding and response to this measure?
7. What is your response to the multiplier effect and Benson's encouragement to spend rather than save in the context of a crisis?
8. Where have you seen the effects of government stimulus? How has it affected you personally?
9. Where has this chapter left you in terms of trusting God for economic outcomes?

Chapter 10: When Disaster Strikes—Reflective Questions

1. The author describes some of the financial hardship in her community in the Philippines. What financial hardship have you experienced in the pandemic, or other times of crisis?
2. Some churches have a triumphalistic theology. How has the theology of your church or background helped or hindered you in responding to your own situation (or time of crisis)?
3. Lament is both grief and protest. What would you like to say in a lament?
4. The apocalyptic writing summons us to be aware and awake. In what ways are you responding to this call?
5. How do you see your ability to endure, to "stay in the pain"?
6. In what ways have you seen God amidst suffering?
7. Where have you found places or experiences of hope?

Chapter 11: Hope in a World in Crisis —Reflective Questions

1. How do you relate to the Narnia stories as a picture of God's immanence?
2. In what way do you have a "closet," a place of prayer to meet with God?
3. Can you see how God invites you back from the "imaginary safe place" to engagement in the real world?
4. How has Galilea's quote become real in your life: "[Christian hope] changes the meaning of life, our way of living, of dying, of acting, and the value we give to all things. Christian hope, like faith and charity, is incarnated in life"?
5. How do you relate to the idea that the Beatitudes are God's promises? Which ones stand out for you as promises?
6. How have you experienced the community of God's people through this crisis, with the church not meeting physically?
7. In what ways are you able to be an icon of hope to other people?
8. Galilea said: "Hope flourishes when it is practiced, when one acts as if its promises were real." In what ways is this true in your life?

Appendix 2

Some Rich Resources

For those who are happy to do some exploring within the Christian faith tradition, here are some rich resources you may wish to engage in order to deepen your reflections and your meditative or contemplative practices:

St. Augustine. *The Confessions.* Translated by Maria Boulding. Hyde Park, NY: New City, 2001.

Bernard of Clairvaux: Selected Works. Edited by Emilie Griffin. New York: HarperSanFrancisco, 2005.

Ilia Delio. *Franciscan Prayer.* Cincinnati: St. Anthony Messenger, 2004.

Hildegard of Bingen: Selections from Her Writings. Edited by Emilie Griffin. New York: HarperSanFrancisco, 2005.

Julian of Norwich. *Revelations of Divine Love.* Translated by Clifton Wolters. London: Penguin, 1966.

Bernard McGinn, ed. *The Essential Writings of Christian Mysticism.* New York: The Modern Library, 2006.

J. Philip Newell. *Celtic Treasure: Daily Scriptures and Prayers.* Norwich, UK: Canterbury, 2005.

The Desert Fathers. Translated by Helen Waddell. New York: Vintage, 1998.

Bibliography

Allen, Diogenes. *Spiritual Theology: The Theology of Yesterday for Spiritual Help Today.* Cambridge, MA: Cowley, 1997.

Amadeo, Kimberly. "US National Debt by Year Compared to GDP and Major Events." *The Balance.* https://www.thebalance.com/national-debt-by-year-compared-to-gdp-and-major-events-3306287.

Andrews, Dave. *Plan Be.* Milton Keynes, UK: Authentic Media, 2008.

Asian Theological Seminary. "ATS Teams Go to Disaster Areas." *InTouch,* 2014. https://issuu.com/atsconnect/docs/ats_yolanda_update-ecopy.

Australian Churches Refugee Taskforce. "Protecting the Lonely Children." 2014. https://humanrights.gov.au/sites/default/files/Submission%20No%20189%20-%20Australian%20Churches%20Refugee%20Taskforce.pdf.

Australian Government Data. "Australian National Debt Explained—With Real Time Debt Clock." *Commodity.com.* https://commodity.com/debt-clock/australia.

Baker, H. Gaylon. *The Cross of Reality.* Minneapolis: AugsburgFortress, 2015.

Barclay, William. *Gospel of Matthew: Volume 1, The Daily Study Bible.* Edinburgh: Saint Andrews, 1956.

Berry, Wendell. *The Long Legged House.* Berkeley, CA: Counterpoint, 2012.

Blainey, Geoffrey. *A Short History of Christianity.* Camberwell, VIC: Viking, 2011.

Bonhoeffer, Dietrich. *The Cost of Discipleship.* London: SCM, 2015.

Brown, Brené. *The Power of Vulnerability.* https://www.ted.com/talks/brene_brown_the_power_of_vulnerability?language=en.

Brueggemann, Walter. "From Hurt to Joy, From Death to Life." *Interpretation* 28 (1974) 3–19.

———. "Psalms and the Life of Faith: A Suggested Typology of Function." *Journal for the Study of the Old Testament* 17 (1980) 3–32.

———. *Theology of the Old Testament: Testimony, Dispute, Advocacy.* Minneapolis: Fortress, 1997.

Butler, Dom Cuthbert. *Western Mysticism.* Mineola, NY: Dover, 2003.

Carlyle, Thomas. "Occasional Discourse on the Negro Question." *Fraser's Magazine for Town and Country* 40 (1849) 670–79.

Carson, Timothy. *Liminal Reality and Transformational Power*. Lanham, MD: University Press of America, 1997.

Chotiner, Isaac. "How Pandemics Change History." *The New Yorker,* March 3, 2020. https://www.newyorker.com/news/q-and-a/how-pandemics-change-history.

Cohn, Robert. *The Shape of Sacred Space: Four Biblical Studies.* American Academy of Religion Studies in Religion 23. Chico, CA: Scholars, 1981.

Collins, Jim. *Good to Great: Why Some Companies Make the Leap . . . and Others Don't.* New York: HarperBusiness, 2001.

Conradie, Ernst M. *Christianity and Earthkeeping: In Search of an Inspiring Vision.* Stellenbosch, SA: Sun, 2011.

Cosby, N. *By Grace Transformed: Christianity for a New Millennium.* New York: Crossroad, 1999.

Crossan, John Dominic. *The Greatest Prayer.* New York: HarperOne, 2010.

de Waal, Esther, ed. *The Celtic Vision.* Liguori, MO: Liguori, 1988.

Delio, Ilia. *Franciscan Prayer.* Cincinnati: St Anthony Messenger, 2004.

Dickson, John. *Humilitas: A Lost Key to Life, Love, and Leadership.* Grand Rapids: Zondervan, 2011.

Dukas, Helen, and Banesh Hoffman. *Albert Einstein, The Human Side: Glimpses from His Archives.* Princeton, NJ: Princeton University Press, 1979.

The Economist. "The pandemic will recast America's health-care industrial complex." *The Economist,* May 5, 2020. https://www.economist.com/business/2020/05/09/the-pandemic-will-recast-americas-health-care-industrial-complex.

Edwards, Denis. *How God Acts.* Hindmarsh: ATF, 2010.

Ellul, Jacques. *The Presence of the Kingdom.* New York: Seabury, 1967.

———. *What I Believe.* London: Eerdmans, 1989.

Flexsenhar, Michael. "How Ancient Christians responded to pandemics." https://blog.oup.com/2020/05/how-ancient-christians-responded-to-pandemics/.

Fogelman, Alex. "Fear as a Lack of Faith?" *Church Life Journal* (2020). https://churchlifejournal.nd.edu/articles/fear-as-a-lack-of-faith/.

Foreign Policy. "Australia: 27 Years of Economic Growth and Counting." https://foreignpolicy.com/sponsored/australia-27-years-of-economic-growth-and-counting/.

Friedman, Thomas L. "We Need Herd Immunity from Trump and the Coronavirus." *New York Times,* April 25, 2020. https://www.nytimes.com/2020/04/25/opinion/coronavirus-immunity-trump.html.

Galilea, Segundo. *The Beatitudes: To Evangelize as Jesus Did.* Translated by Robert R. Barr. Maryknoll, NY: Orbis, 1984.

———. *Following Jesus.* Translated by H. Phillips. Maryknoll, NY: Orbis, 1981.

———. *A Spirituality of Hope.* Translated by Terrence Cambias. Maryknoll, NY: Orbis, 1988.

———. *The Way of Living Faith.* Translated by John W. Diercksmeier. San Francisco: Harper and Row, 1988.

Gillard, Richard. "The Servant Song." © Richard Gillard. 1977. Universal music.

Goldingay, John. "The Dynamic Cycle of Praise and Prayer in the Psalms." *Journal for the Study of the Old Testament* 20 (1981) 85–90.

Gorman, Michael J. *Participating in Christ: Exploring in Paul's Theology and Spirituality.* Grand Rapids: Baker Academic, 2019.

Gorospe, Athena. *Narrative and Identity: An Ethical Reading of Exodus 4.* Leiden: Brill, 1997.

———. "Old Testament Narratives in Context: Moses' Reverse Migration and a Hermeneutics of Possibility." In *The Gospel in Culture: Contextualization Issues through Asian Eyes*, edited by Melba Maggay, 191–97. Mandaluyong City, Philippines: OMF, 2013.

Green, Michael, and Paul Stevens. *New Testament Spirituality: True Discipleship and Spiritual Maturity*. Guildford, UK: Eagle, 1994.

Grenz, Stanley J. *Theology for the Community of God*. Grand Rapids: Eerdmans, 2000.

Hayachi, Gary. Living Waters seminar.

Hinton, Thomas "Health expenditure as percentage of the gross domestic product (GDP) in Australia from 2006 to 2017." *Statista*. https://www.statista.com/statistics/628582/australia-health.

Holt, Bradley P. *Thirsty for God: A Brief History of Christian Spirituality*. Minneapolis: Augsburg, 1993.

International Ministries. "A Reflection on Disorientating Events: Orientation, Disorientation, Reorientation." https://www.internationalministries.org/a-reflection-on-disorientating-events-orientation-disorientation-and-reorientation/.

Jeske, Christine. "This Pandemic Hits Americans Where We're Spiritually Weak." *Christianity Today* 64 (2020). https://www.christianitytoday.com/ct/2020/may-web-only/coronavirus-pandemic-hits-americans-spiritually-weak.html.

Johnson, Luke T. *Faith's Freedom: A Classic Spirituality for Contemporary Christians*. Minneapolis: Fortress, 1990.

Jones, Stanley E. *Christ and Human Suffering*. London: Hodder & Stoughton, 1933.

Kelly, Paul. "Coronavirus: Whatever it Takes must be our Motto." *The Weekend Australian*, Inquirer, March 21, 2020, 21.

Ladd, George E. *A Theology of the New Testament*. London: Lutterworth, 1975.

Lamentations Bible Project. https://www.youtube.com/watch?v=p8GDFPdaQZQ.

Leunig, Michael. "The Leunig Fragments" 43.07 https://iview.abc.net.au/show/leunig-fragments.

———. "The World is Changing." https://www.leunig.com.au/works/recent-cartoons/1031-the-world-is-changing.

Lewis, C. S. *The Lion, the Witch, and the Wardrobe*. New York: Harper Collins, 1994.

Loyola Press. "Icons as Religious Art." https://www.loyolapress.com/catholic-resources/family/catholic-teens/religious-art/icons-as-religious-art/.

Luther, Martin. *Luther's Works*, vol. 21. St. Louis: Concordia, 1968.

———. *Luther's Works*, vol. 24. St. Louis: Concordia, 1961.

Manzanilla-Manalo, Annabel. "Psycho-Spiritual Support in the Aftermath of Super-typhoon Yolanda/Haiyan." *InTouch* (April 2014). https://issuu.com/atsconnect/docs/ats_yolanda_update-ecopy.

Martin, Roger. "Changing the Mind of the Corporation." *Harvard Business Review*. September-October 1993. https://hbr.org/1993/11/changing-the-mind-of-the-corporation.

May, Gerald G. *Simply Sane: The Spirituality of Mental Health*. New York: Crossroad, 1993.

Merton, Thomas. *No Man is an Island*. Boston: Shambhala, 2005.

Mikulic, Martej. "U.S. national health expenditure as percent of GDP from 1960 to 2020." *Statista*. https://www.statista.com/statistics/184968/us-health-expenditure-as-percent-of-gdp-since-1960/.

Milgate, Wesley, ed. *Together in Song: Australian Hymnbook*. Melbourne: Harper-Collins-Religious, 1999.

Minear, Paul S. *Matthew: The Teacher's Gospel*. London: Darton, Longman and Todd, 1982.

Molito, Alvin M. "God in the Face of the Other: A Biblical Model for Resolving Conflicts." In *How Long, O Lord?: The Challenge and Promise of Reconciliation and Peace*, edited by Athena E. Gorospe and Charles R. Ringma, 43–58. Carlisle, Cumbria: Langham Global Library, 2018.

Newell, John Philip. *Celtic Treasure: Daily Scriptures and Prayer.* Grand Rapids: Eerdmans, 2005.

Niebuhr, H. Richard. *Christ and Culture.* New York: Harper, 1975.

Norris, Kathleen. *Acedia & Me: A Marriage, Monks, and a Writer's Life.* New York: Riverhead, 2008.

Northumbria Community. *Celtic Daily Prayer.* San Francisco: HarperOne, 2000.

Nouwen, Henri J. M. *In the House of the Lord: The Journey from Fear to Love.* New York: Doubleday, 1986.

Official Gazette. "The Anti-Terrorism Act of 2020." https://www.officialgazette.gov.ph/downloads/2020/06jun/20200703-RA-11479-RRD.pdf.

Osborne, Albert. "My life must be." Salvation Army Hymnary. https://hymnary/org/hymn/SBSA1986/512.

Page, Scott E. *The Diversity Bonus: How Great Teams Pay Off in the Knowledge Economy.* Princeton, NJ: Princeton University Press, 2018.

———. *The Model Thinker: What You Need to Know to Make Data Work for You.* New York: Basic, 2018.

Peterson, Eugene. *Leap Over a Wall.* New York: Harper, 1997.

Plantinga, Cornelius. *Not the Way It's Supposed to Be: A Breviary of Sin.* Grand Rapids: Eerdmans, 1996.

Pohl, Christine D. *Making Room: Recovering Hospitality as a Christian Tradition.* Grand Rapids: Eerdmans, 1999.

Rah, Soong-Chan. *Prophetic Lament: A Call for Justice in Troubled Times.* Downers Grove, IL: InterVarsity, 2015.

Rasmussen, Larry L. *Earth-Honoring Faith: Religious Ethics in a New Key.* Oxford: Oxford University Press, 2012.

Ringma, Charles R. *Hear the Ancient Wisdom.* Eugene, OR: Cascade, 2013.

———. *Let My People Go with Martin Luther King, Jr.* Vancouver: Regent College Publishing, 2009.

———. *Seek the Silences with Thomas Merton.* Vancouver: Regent College Publishing, 2013.

Ringma, Charles, and Irene Alexander, eds. *Of Martyrs, Monks, and Mystics.* Eugene, OR: Cascade, 2015.

Robinson, Bernard P. "Zipporah to the Rescue: A Contextual Study of Exodus 4:2–46," *Vetus Testamentum* 36, (1986) 447–58.

Robinson, Georgina. "Rudd's Stimulus Package: What will you get?" *The Sydney Morning Herald.* February 4, 2009. https://www.smh.com.au/national/rudds-stimulus-package-what-you-will-get-20090204-gdtc9a.html.

Rohr, Richard. *True Self, False Self.* Tape series. Cincinnati: St Antony Messenger, n.d.

Römer, Thomas. "De l'Archaïque au Subversif: Le cas d'Exode 4/24-26." *Etudes Theologiques et Religieuses* 69 (1994) 1–12.

Ross, Maggie. *Pillars of Flame: Power, Priesthood and Spiritual Maturity.* San Francisco: Harper & Row, 1988.

Safa, Mohamad, permanent representative at the United Nations. @mhdksafa—Mar 21, 2020. https://twitter.com/mhdksafa/status/1241069931002826754?lang=en.

Smith, Aaron. *Slums Reimagined: How Informal Settlements Help the Poor Overcome Poverty.* Skyforest, CA: Urban Loft, 2020.

Society of St. Francis. *Celebrating Common Prayer.* Harrisburg, PA: Morehouse, 1994.

Stark, Rodney. *The Rise of Christianity: How the Obscure, Marginal Jesus Movement Became the Dominant Religious Force in the Western World in a Few Centuries.* New York: HarperSan Francisco, 1997.

Statista. "U.S. national health expenditure as percent of GDP from 1960 to 2020." https://www.statista.com/statistics/184968/us-health-expenditure-as-percent-of-gdp-since-1960/.

Steere, Douglas. *Gleanings: A Random Harvest.* Nashville: Upper Room, 1986.

Taizé Reflections. "O Lord Hear my Prayer." https://www.youtube.com/watch?v=WTuFglyOQvI.

Thompson, Curt. *Anatomy of the Soul: Surprising Connections between Neuroscience and Spiritual Practices that can Transform your Life and Relationships.* Carol Stream, IL: Tyndale, 2010.

Tolkien, J. R. R. *On Fairy Stories*, edited by Verlyn Flieger and Douglas A. Anderson. London: HarperCollins 2014.

Trading Economics. "Japan General Government Gross Debt to GDP." https://tradingeconomics.com/japan/government-debt-to-gdp.

Turner, Victor. *The Forest of Symbols: Aspects of Ndembu Ritual.* Ithaca, NY: Cornell University Press, 1967.

———. *The Ritual Process: Structure and Anti-structure.* Chicago: Aldine, 1969.

Tyson, Paul. *Returning to Reality: Christian Platonism for Our Times.* Eugene, OR: Cascade, 2014.

Underhill, Evelyn. *The Augusten Books of Poetry.* London: Ernest Benn, 1932.

United Nations. "The Climate Crisis: A Race We Can Win." https://www.un.org/en/un75/climate-crisis-race-we-can-win.

van Gennep, Arnold. *The Rites of Passage.* Translated by Monika B. Vizedom and Gabrielle L. Caffee. Chicago: University of Chicago Press, 1960.

Villanueva, Federico G. *The Uncertainty of Hearing: A Study of the Sudden Change of Mood in the Psalms of Lament.* Supplements to Vetus Testamentum 21. Leiden: Brill, 2008.

Williams, Andrew. "Biblical Lament and Political Protest." *Cambridge Papers* (2014) 23. https://www.jubilee-centre.org/cambridge-papers/biblical-lament-political-protest-andrew-williams.

Williams, Rowan. *The Wound of Knowledge.* London: Darton, Longman and Todd, 1990.

———. *Where God Happens: Discovering Christ in One Another.* Boston: New Seeds, 2005.

Wink, Walter. *The Powers That Be: Theology for a New Millennium.* New York: Doubleday, 1998.

Wong, Siqi. ""Angels in yellow': Christians in Wuhan take to the streets to boldly spread love, share Christ." February 10, 2020. https://thir.st/blog/christians-in-wuhan-boldly-share-christ-spread-love-on-streets/.

Wright, N. T. "Christianity Offers No Answers About the Coronavirus. It's Not Supposed To." *Time*, March 29, 2020. https://time.com/5808495/coronavirus/christianity/.

Wuest, Tom. "Breath of God." In *Burn this as a Light.* 2016.

Yaconelli, Mark. *Contemplative Youth Ministry.* El Cajon, CA: Youth Specialities, 2006.

Name Index

Subject Index

www.ingramcontent.com/pod-product-compliance
Lightning Source LLC
Chambersburg PA
CBHW031432150426
43191CB00006B/478
* 9 7 8 1 7 2 5 2 8 9 5 5 0 *